Grace TO ESCAPE

Domestic Violence

LINDA JOHNSON

Grace to Escape: Domestic Violence
by Linda Johnson

Copyright © 2013 by Linda Johnson
All Rights Reserved

ISBN: 978-0-9890800-0-2

Published by Linda Johnson | P.O. Box 79281 | Fort Worth, TX 76179

Editorial by Jordan Media Services | P.O. Box 761593 | Fort Worth, TX USA
www.jordanmediaservices.com

Typesetting/Layout by Ken Fraser Designs | grafxedge@gmail.com

Printed in the United States of America

Contents

Dedication

Acknowledgements

Preface

Epilogue

Final Thoughts

Dedication

I dedicate this book to my sons, Jason and Joel (names were changed to protect the innocent), who suffered alongside me, yet lived to see God bring each of us through in total victory. I love you both more than you will ever know, and every day I continue to commit to being the very best mom I can possibly be.

This book is also dedicated to the hundreds of thousands of spouses, both women and men, who daily face the pains from abusive marriages, and fight relentlessly, sometimes to the death, to escape. And to the children who are victimized as a result. I applaud your courage.

Acknowledgements

I don't know how many times I listened as Jason and Joel firmly urged and encouraged: "Mom, you have to write our story so others will know." And so it is through much persuasion from my two wonderful sons that I have written this book.

It has been over twenty-five years since we escaped to freedom on that wintery night of March. We look back on how faithful the Lord was to us throughout, and we continue to celebrate and rejoice in His goodness. He honors those who will put their trust in Him.

Jason and Joel needed to see this victory as much as I did. Was it easy? NO! Many times, the pressure seemed unbearable. We had to keep believing and trusting the Lord. Proverbs 3:5-6 says, "Trust in the Lord with ALL thine heart and lean not unto thine own understanding. In ALL thy ways acknowledge him and he SHALL direct thy paths."

I offer special thanks to my parents, who stuck with us through this ordeal—unselfishly allowing us to stay in the safety of their home for as long as we needed. My mother encouraged me to write down the scriptures God impressed me to stand on for our deliverance and put them in a small spiral notebook. I did exactly that, keeping God's Word and His promise of protection ever close to me. I even took that little spiral recipe book with me to court and secretively read it from inside my purse. I still mediate on those scriptures nearly every day. God's Word sustained us then, and it continues to keep us today.

Thanks to the countless people who prayed for us all across the nation. I may not know you all by name, but you know who you are. We so appreciate all the money that was sent our way when we needed it the most. At times it came in the mail, other times it was handed to us. Once, an envelope containing money was taped anonymously to our front door. Support also came by way of food, clothing, and other items. We are so grateful!

Thanks, also, to my many friends for praying for this book project. I appreciate your loyal friendship and support. You are a special treasure to me. Agreement in prayer really works, according to Matthew 18:18-19.

My editors were amazing! They were there to push this project through to completion. With their help, it has been a most enjoyable journey for me.

Finally, I am thankful to the Lord for allowing me to write this book. The Bible says in Hebrews 10:38, "The just shall live by faith." Through faith in His Word, God delivered my children and me. God is not a respecter of persons, but He is a respecter of faith. It thrills my heart to be able to put these victories down on paper.

God is good ALL the time (Psalm 145:9)! And yes, something good did happen to us. He made a way of escape! And today, as always, I hold up the Word spoken in Joshua 24:15 and declare: "As for me and my house, we will serve the Lord!"

Preface

The screams had all but become familiar.

Like clockwork, they happened nearly every night as Jason, thirteen, awakened to the fear that his father was trying to kill him. Of course, it wasn't true. But the dreams were real. Just as real as what had happened five years earlier when my ex-husband held a loaded gun to our son's neck and threatened to pull the trigger.

And he was serious!

Jason's screams were not the only ones often breaking the silence of the night in our home. Mine were less obvious, as were the tears that soaked my pillow many nights as I cried myself to sleep. But they were there just the same, and for much the same reason. Sometimes I wanted to just stay in bed and pull the covers over my head, hoping things would be different in the morning.

My marriage had gone bad. Not over time, but from the very beginning when, after only two weeks my husband looked at me and said: "I wish I had never married you." And it would get progressively worse as time went on. Much worse!

I wish this were my story alone to tell. The truth is, I am not alone. We are not alone. Statistics reveal that hundreds of thousands each year face the pain and agony that result from spousal abuse. Women and men! Children suffer as well. And in the majority of those cases, the helpless victims never find a way out.

Out of respect for those involved, and because I do not wish to bring shame or dishonor to them or their names, I have changed the identities of all parties and locales were not mentioned.

Our struggle lasted for nearly fourteen years.

The physical and mental scars we bear, and reminders of a ten-year custody battle, serve to remind us—every day—of the pain, the agony, the torment we endured.

But today, we are free.

With God's help, I found a way of escape—for me, and for my two sons. You are not alone. And after reading this book, I believe you, too, will have found your way to escape!

This is my story …

Chapter 1

❦

A Plan and a Purpose

The sun was just setting over what had been the last few days of winter as I loaded the last of my possessions onto the backseat and into the trunk of the car. A few more trips inside the house and I'd be done.

Done!

That word resounded in my head with a thud similar to that of a splashing ocean wave crashing against the side of a rocky cliff. It reverberated like an echo bouncing back at me from deep within the recesses of a wide canyon.

Done! Finished! Over! No more!

That was where I saw myself as I rushed to get away—to escape the pain and hurt of yet another marriage gone sour and a husband so brutally vicious that he had threatened not only my life, but the lives of our two small children. I was walking— no, I was running away from a nightmare—four years of what I thought had to have been the worst marriage relationship any person could ever have endured.

I was fleeing for our lives!

Hindsight is always 20/20.

How many times have I heard that one?

The truth is, looking back, I really should have known better.

Even as a child, I was what you might consider a person of faith. I learned early in life what it meant to live for God, to trust Him for whatever I needed, and to always obey His Word. A verse of scripture on a plaque that hung on the wall in my bedroom had been indelibly engraved on my heart. It read: "Be not afraid, only believe" (Mark 5:36). The scripture in the Bible from Matthew 6:33 was not foreign to me: "But seek ye first the kingdom of God, and his righteousness; and all these things shall be added unto you."

I had remembered that verse from my early years after becoming a Christian. And I believed that God would do just what that verse said: that as I sought Him, as I determined to live right and do what His Word commanded, He would see that I was always taken care of—that I would be given the desires of my heart.

I also knew how to treat others with kindness and respect. So, I could not have imagined that I would ever do anything to, or against, my husband that would cause our marriage to break up. What I didn't consider though, was that it didn't have to be ME who would cause our marriage to fail. I never considered that the man I loved just may not have loved me—or that he didn't love me enough to fight to keep our marriage together.

In the past twelve years, I had been married twice. Both times, I thought I married for love—and that the men I married loved me. I was so wrong!

Now that hindsight had kicked in, I realized that I didn't HAVE to get married. I WANTED to be married. I now knew that each time what I had convinced myself were leadings from the Lord to get married—seemingly marked with His stamp of approval—were actually enticements of my own flesh. Both times, I yielded to my own selfish desires. And that's where my troubles began.

If someone had told me as a young child that I would someday be twice divorced, no doubt I would have thought they were out of their mind. Me? Married and divorced twice! How ridiculous does that sound?

Worse yet, had they said my marriages would end because of emotional, verbal, or physical abuse, that would have been even more shocking.

I won't say I sat around planning how my life would turn out, dreaming that someday Mr. Right would come along, sweep me off my feet and whisk me away to a world filled with love, joy, and pleasure. Yes, I wanted to be married, to have children, and live happily ever after. What girl in her right mind doesn't? As a Christian, I loved the thought of sharing my life with the man I loved—perhaps even being partners in ministry and sharing the love of God and winning the lost to Jesus.

Instead, as a young mother in my thirties with two small children, that wasn't the case. There I was again, divorced and about to start life over for a third time.

How did I get to this place in my life?

What did I do that was so terribly wrong that, despite my faith in God, despite everything I had learned about His loving-kindness, I would wind up disappointed, wounded, and divorced, on the end of two failed marriages? I had been a good wife, and a good mother. And I was faithful.

But things happen—things that are sometimes beyond our control. And when they do, many times we suffer the consequences.

Looking to the Future

The going down of the sun marked the end of the day. In a few hours, there would be another. And that's where my mind was. Remembering the words of Apostle Paul in Philippians 3:13, I was trying hard to forget about the things from my past—the things that were now behind me. I had made a conscious decision to move forward, and was focusing on the future. I didn't know what the Lord had in store for me and my two sons, but whatever it was, I believed it had to be good.

But a decision to move forward, to forget those things that are in your past, doesn't necessarily mean those things are automatically erased from your memory, or your history. The truth is, they aren't. Much like residue, they linger in the recesses of your mind, and they tend to pop up at very strategic moments and in very uncomfortable ways because they really are very much a part of your life history.

And if there are others who were in some way affected by what you endured, those things are still very much a part of their history, too. They remember them just as much, and perhaps even as often as you.

That's a big part of why I decided to write this book.

When I think of marriage, I view it from the perspective that I believe God intended when He made Adam and Eve. Marriage was created out of God's love and compassion for mankind. But it was also instituted out of His desire to see that man was never alone—that he would always have someone at his side, someone to share his thoughts and visions, his ups and downs, his feelings. The Bible helps us to see that in Genesis, chapter 2:

> God said, It is not good that the man should be alone; I will make him an help meet for him…And the LORD God caused a deep sleep to fall upon Adam, and he slept: and he took one of his ribs, and closed up the flesh instead thereof; and the rib, which the LORD God had taken from man, made he a woman, and brought her unto the man. And Adam said, This is now bone of my bones, and flesh of my flesh: she shall be called Woman, because she was taken out of Man (vv. 18, 21-23).

I am not the first person ever to experience spousal abuse, and unfortunately I won't be the last. Domestic violence is considered one of the most pressing issues in American society today. According to an article published in May 2012 by the National Coalition Against Domestic Violence, 1.3 million women are assaulted by their partners every year. The article reported that while 85 percent of domestic violence reported is against women, the Center for Disease Control found in a conflicting survey taken two years earlier in 2010 that 40 percent of the victims of severe, physical domestic violence are men.

Those are staggering and alarming figures. Yet, when you consider the condition the nation is in today regarding marriage, morals, and family values, while they are not acceptable figures they are certainly understandable.

If you're reading this book, then possibly you're currently a victim of domestic violence. You've been hurt or abused, and you're looking for a way out—a way to escape! The message of this book is a simple one: There is help for you. The Lord is there to help you through the pain and agony of this, and anything else

When I returned home from camp, I was literally on fire for God. I never knew I could be so hungry for any one thing, especially God, but I was. My desire to learn more about Him just kept growing. So, my family and I joined a church where that could happen.

The leaders in my new home church recognized my spiritual zeal as well, and took advantage of it by asking me to assume the leadership of our youth by putting on a church musical production, which I wrote and produced. Most importantly, though, we saw people, young and old, get excited about knowing, loving, and serving the Lord.

The Challenge of College Life

I went to college, which was one of the best times I can remember. Unlike junior and senior high school, college presented a completely different set of challenges for me, but with a more mature group of people which is to be expected.

Though the school I attended was not right there in my hometown, I was excited as I nervously contemplated and anticipated what it would be like—how different it would be—from high school. But I was up for the challenge. I was ready to take on the world of the unknown and everything that came with it. I was excited about becoming a college freshman.

College was everything I had hoped, and expected, it would be—at least from the perspective of my Christian walk. To say that I was more interested in my relationship with the Lord and learning more about Him than I was with actual school work, would be an understatement. But that's not why I went to college. I was there to get an education, so I was diligent to be faithful regarding academics. I was highly competitive, and I still am to this day. One of my crowning achievements back then was winning first place in the college state leadership competition and going on to compete in the national competition. I was interviewed by the local television network, where I got the opportunity to share my faith and how it helped me win.

When I graduated from college, one of the first things I did was get a job so I could pay off my government student loan.

When I bought my first car, I was able to pay for it with cash that I had diligently saved over a period of time.

A Taste of Persecution

Up until now, much of what you've read regarding my experiences as a Christian has been good. I wish that were the case with all that is to follow in these pages. Sadly, it's not.

Tests. Trials. Persecution.

They are all part of the Christian life. Jesus made that clear when He told His disciples, "If they have persecuted me, they will also persecute you" (John 15:20). Life as a Christian was so good to me that I never really ever gave thought to things like tests and trials. I soon found out, though, that they were real and that they were waiting for me—big time!

I got my first taste of persecution during spring break, when a group of believers converged on Daytona Beach, Florida. Our sole task, as we dispersed along the beach, was to witness to people and invite them to receive Jesus as Lord and Savior. One night as we were canvassing a group of people, a young man put a knife to my throat and said, "I could kill you." Almost instantly, I responded: "Yes, you could kill me. But then, you would never hear about my Jesus."

Slowly, the man dropped the knife and retreated.

That same night, his girlfriend gave her life to the Lord.

I also received what could be considered my first "attack" from the enemy during that same trip when I nearly drowned.

It was my first experience ever being near the ocean, and I had been thinking how grateful I was that I knew how to swim. Several of us had gone for a swim in a shallow portion of the ocean when suddenly, I was snatched up by a strong wave and swept out into deeper water. A young man from our group named Steve, tried to help get me back to shallow water, but with each wave that rushed ashore, we both were being taken farther and farther out into the ocean.

Suddenly, a man on a raft appeared seemingly out of nowhere and rescued Steve and me, and got us back to shore. By this time I was unresponsive, but I could hear people around me talking and someone calling for an ambulance. The only thing I have a very vivid remembrance of is that the man on the raft placed his hand on my shoulder and whispered: "Jesus will pull you through."

Afterwards, the man vanished in the crowd and none of us ever saw him again.

Days later, when my parents met me at the airport upon my arrival back home, I shared with them about the swimming incident.

Not sounding surprised at all, my mother said rather unassumingly: "It happened on Friday afternoon."

Then she told me that she had been doing the dishes on that day when she sensed my life was in danger. She prayed that I would live and not die.

I've heard many stories about people falling into peril only to have some mysterious person suddenly appear and save them. In the natural, such things sound ridiculous, but when you understand the Lord and how He protects and provides for His people, it's not difficult to believe He would send an angel to rescue you. To this day, I am convinced God sent an angel to save me from drowning.

That experience deepened my love and hunger for God and increased my desire to serve Him in whatever way I could. To satisfy that hunger, I joined an evangelism team—a move that eventually led me to "the man of my dreams."

Or, so I thought.

———— ❧ ————

Pray this prayer:

Dear Father, I love You because You first loved me, and You proved Your love by sending Your Son, Jesus, to be the Sacrifice for my sins — crucified on the cross — so that I can live through Him. I diligently study and meditate Your Word by the help and guidance of Your Holy Spirit within me. My heart's desire is continually to learn more about You and tell others about You. I ask for Your wisdom, expecting to know what to do in every situation. I give all my worries and cares to You because You care about what happens to me. I am so thankful because no matter what happens, You keep me safe, and You give me victory, in Jesus' name. Amen.

Scriptures for Meditation: John 15:20; Romans 13:8; John 19:18-19; 1 John 4:10, 19; 2 Timothy 2:15; 1 Peter 5:7 NLT; Psalm 119:117; 1 Corinthians 15:57 AMP; James 1:5; Romans 10:9-13

Chapter 3

❧

Mr. Right? Wrong!

Our evangelism team was a fairly diverse group that included both young teens and adults. There were a few parents in the group who for whatever reason, had decided I would be a nice catch for their sons, and didn't hesitate to make their thoughts and feelings known. Needless to say, there were offers for me to go out on dates.

That's how I met Roger.

Remember what I said earlier about hindsight being 20/20? Well, this is one of those cases.

I don't know that I was overly attracted to Roger, although there was a certain mystique about him that I didn't see in any of the other guys in our church. I don't know why, but the fact that he and I shared the same birthday caught my attention. Others thought, and convinced me, that that was God's way of telling me He had set Roger apart expressly for me. Roger was interested in the things of the Lord, too. So when he proposed, I accepted.

Looking back, it was not my nature or character to get so caught up in the moment and make decisions without first consulting God. Even though I was still what some might consider a "baby Christian," I considered myself smart enough to know when to go to God about a matter.

Maybe Roger was God-sent. But I should have at least given the Lord the opportunity to confirm that he was, and that I wasn't just dreaming the whole thing up because I wanted what others around me had.

The truth is, that's exactly what I was doing.

The warning signs were all around—becoming clearer and clearer. But I refused to acknowledge them.

One sign that this marriage was not to be was when I broke off the engagement and gave Roger back his ring shortly after we became engaged. I wasn't comfortable with my quick decision and, as it turned out, neither was he. However, it wasn't long before Roger had a change of heart. His charm, his eloquence, and his enticing words lured me back into his arms, and before I knew it I was headed for the altar.

There was a second warning as well, that actually came on my wedding day as I was preparing to walk down the aisle. It wasn't an audible voice, but it was one that I heard clearly, deep down in my heart. And I knew it was the Lord.

I heard Him say to me, "It is not too late to say no."

Lord, are You kidding me? It's my wedding day. I'm about to be married. What do You mean, "It's not too late to say no"? What would people think? I've never heard of anyone with a church filled with wedding guests change their mind about getting married.

Those were my very thoughts.

Not surprisingly, I didn't get an answer from the Lord.

I didn't need one. The Lord had already said what He wanted to say. Now, it was up to me to obey. If only I could have confided in my mother, but I didn't get the chance to say anything to her.

When the preacher asked if I would take Roger to be my lawful wedded husband, everything in me wanted to respond: "No!" Instead, I went through the motions. I said "Yes." And the ceremony continued. On the outside I was smiling—showing the kind of joy one would expect to see on the face of a kid who had just received a brand-new toy. On the inside, I was hurting and confused because I knew what I had just done was wrong, that I had made a serious mistake. I wanted to take it back. I wanted to hit "delete" and undo the entire last thirty minutes of my life. I wanted to run out of the church, to get as far away as possible from all the well-wishers and their congratulatory smiles, hugs, and handshakes, and never look back.

Chapter 4

❧❧❧❧

First Things First—ALWAYS!

*T*he Bible says in Proverbs 14:12, "There is a way which seemeth right unto a man, but the end thereof are the ways of death." The *New Living Translation* says it this way: "There is a path before each person that seems right, but it ends in death."

You don't need a degree in rocket science to understand those words. It's pretty clear what the Lord is saying here. I don't know that I've ever met anyone who didn't have some idea about what he or she wanted out of life. Either they had already decided what they were going to do and were working to make it happen, or they had a pretty good idea. The question is, was God included in their planning? Were they moving according to His will, or were they proceeding based on choices they made on their own?

There IS a way that SEEMS right. And most of us are familiar with it, because we've experienced it at one time or another.

It starts in our head, not our heart. And it's based on our thoughts, feelings, and desires, rather than hearing the voice of God. Yet, His Word plainly tells us that He has a plan for our life, and that it is a good plan that ensures our prosperity and well-being.

Making Right Choices

The Bible has some very revealing things to say about the kinds of choices we make, and our thoughts about those choices.

In Deuteronomy 30:19, for example, the Lord says, "I call heaven and earth to record this day against you, that I have set before you life and death, blessing and cursing: therefore choose life, that both thou and thy seed may live."

In a sense, this could be considered God's way of teaching us about making choices. Only here, He gives us a little help. He gives us a choice, and then He tells us which to choose.

"Choose life!"

Choose blessing.

Why does He do that? Because that's where we find Him—in His will to bless us. That's where we find all that He has for us.

The problem is, most people don't understand that. They believe they're capable of making their own decisions, their own choices. Consequently, they leave God out—not knowing or considering the fact that wrong choices on their part can result in being cursed, or worse, destroyed.

Isaiah 55:6-9, tells us:

Seek ye the LORD while he may be found, call ye upon him while he is near: Let the wicked forsake his way, and the unrighteous man his thoughts: and let him return unto the Lord, and he will have mercy upon him; and to our God, for he will abundantly pardon. For my thoughts are not your thoughts, neither are your ways my ways, saith the Lord. For as the heavens are higher than the earth, so are my ways higher than your ways, and my thoughts than your thoughts.

Some may look at this passage and immediately point out that it is addressing the wicked or unrighteous man. They might say, "But that's not me. I'm a born-again believer who loves God with all my heart."

Certainly, I didn't see myself as wicked or unrighteous. I loved God, and I knew He loved me. And I believed I was sensitive enough to His Spirit to recognize His voice. What I discovered, though, was that you can love God and still choose to not obey what He tells you to do because it doesn't agree with what you want or desire. That's called disobedience. And disobedience to God and His Word is what gets us believers, and nonbelievers, into trouble.

you would have imagined or planned, but if God is leading you, then follow and obey Him. It may not seem like the quickest, most direct way to reach your goals or your destiny, but take it anyway. The Bible says in Psalm 37:23 that a good man's [or woman's] steps are ordered by the Lord. In this sense, a good man, or woman, is one who is born again and in right relationship with God. Are you a good man or woman? If so, then God has already ordered your steps. He has set your course and established His plan for your life. And it is a good plan. You only need to align your life with His plan, step onto and follow the path He has set for you.

Pray this prayer:

Dear Father, You have given me the freedom and right to make choices. You have kindly encouraged me to make the right decisions and warned me of the consequences of the wrong ones. Unfortunately, I have made some bad ones, erroneously thinking I was right. I confess my disobedience and I ask You to forgive me, and I receive Your promise of forgiveness and Your mercy. I realize and acknowledge that I need Your help. I don't want to make trouble for myself and anyone else, and I certainly have found out that I cannot fix problems — they only get worse. You alone are God — there is no other. I come first to You. You promise to take care of my needs and to give me the desires of my heart. You also promise that as I diligently study, meditate, and obey Your Word, then I make my own way prosperous, I deal wisely, and I have good success, in Jesus' name. Amen.

Scriptures for Meditation: Proverbs 14:12; Deuteronomy 30:19-20; Isaiah 55:6-9; Exodus 3:7-8; Judges 6:1-4, 7-10; John 10:10; Psalm 37:23; Joshua 1:8; 1 John 1:9; Psalm 136:1; Isaiah 43:10,13 AMP; Matthew 6:33; Philippians 4:19; Psalm 37:4

Chapter 5

❧

Preparing for Change

*F*or several years since I had become a Christian, I had a desire to go to Bible school. After searching and praying for the right place, I submitted my application and was accepted. I can't begin to explain the excitement that filled my soul the day the packet arrived with a letter announcing, "You have been accepted!"

When the day finally arrived that I was to leave for Bible school, I was overwhelmed with joy. It was exciting and frightening all at the same time. As I tied down the last of my few pieces of furniture, and arranged my other possessions in the back of my parents' pickup truck, I was excited at the thought of experiencing new surroundings and meeting new people.

Following behind my parents as we drove our vehicles out of the driveway that morning, I sensed in my heart that something good was about to happen. One chapter of my life was ending and a new one was about to begin.

Was my dream really about to become a reality? I wondered.

As the miles clicked off and we continued down the highway, I reflected on my life's journey up to that point, and how I was brought to this major decision to move so far from home. It was more than the "stone's throw" driving distance I had experienced in college, for sure. Yes, I was a young girl leaving home for the very first time. But in a number of ways I was excited to discover what God was about to do in my life.

In that moment I thought about the Lord's servant, Abraham, and how God spoke to him one day and told him to pack his bags and get out of town. The Lord told Abraham:

> "Leave your native country, your relatives, and your
> father's family, and go to the land that I will show you.
> I will make you into a great nation. I will bless you and
> make you famous, and you will be a blessing to others.
> I will bless those who bless you and curse those who
> treat you with contempt. All the families on earth will be
> blessed through you" (Genesis 12:1-3, NLT).

For just a moment, I imagined myself in Abraham's place.

Surely Abraham must have had reservations about leaving his family, his friends, and familiar surroundings behind and going to a place he knew absolutely nothing about. He probably wondered if he was doing the right thing. But, Abraham was a man of faith. He recognized God's voice, and He was always quick to obey whatever God told Him to do. If he did have any doubts or questions, they certainly didn't keep him from obeying God. And because he was obedient, things worked out for him in ways that he would never have imagined.

In a sense, I suppose you could say I heard from God like Abraham did. Otherwise, I don't believe I would have made the decision to go away to Bible school, and I certainly would not have chosen a school so far away from home. But I was in love with God, and I trusted Him.

I really was very excited about what He was doing in my life!

Every morning for me in Bible school was like heaven—being in an atmosphere that was saturated with the Word of God and filled with people who had the same spiritual desires I had. The Word of God was so rich, and so plentiful. I felt like I could never get enough! It was like having my own personal heaven on earth.

My first year in Bible school went by at whirlwind speed, and before I knew it, I was preparing to start my second year. Little did I know that I was also about to experience another "second."

Within weeks of starting classes, I met Greg.

By the end of the first semester, we were married.

That's exactly how quickly it happened.

And, no, I didn't really stop to think long and hard about what I had just come through. In retrospect, I'm sure I gave it some thought. But obviously it wasn't enough to convince myself that this was the wrong thing to do. In fact, I thought it was the RIGHT thing.

Another Surprise Announcement!

Greg was a first-year student when we met at a fall function. I guess you could say it was déjà vu all over again. Just like Roger, he displayed all the right credentials that signaled that he might be sent from God. We both loved God and had a strong passion to be in full-time ministry. Also, just like Roger, he had all the right words to sweep me off my feet in record time!

Two weeks after we were married, Greg looked at me and said he wished he had never married me. I was devastated, and didn't know what I should do. For a moment, my mind flashed back to Roger and the day he asked me to leave home.

Dear God, not again!

Why is this happening to me?

No sooner had he spoken those words, Greg retracted them and asked my forgiveness. We never really discussed it, so I don't know what prompted him to say such a terrible thing in the first place.

Was he testing my love for him or what?

Part of me wanted to know—the other part was too afraid to ask.

I forgave him and never looked back. My hope was that it would never come up again.

In January, we started the second semester of school as a married couple. I was in my second year and Greg was in his first.

As part of my new experience as a Christian, I had heard a lot regarding the prophetic word. Though I had not been a recipient of any particular prophecy, I was always intrigued when a minister spoke out after hearing from God and delivered a specific word to an individual, or to the Body of Christ as a whole.

One day during class, a well-known pastor was ministering when he suddenly stopped, looked in my direction, and asked me to stand.

"I have got an encouraging word for you," he told me.

What he said next was more than just encouragement—it was a word from the Lord that was designed to prepare me for a very rocky future.

"Yes, my daughter, have not I seen you? Do I not know your down sitting and your uprising?" saith the Lord. "You are a mighty woman of valor, because you'll not give up. Yea, I have seen your spirit when the enemy has tried to stop you. And you said, 'No, devil, no devil, you are not going to keep me out of the fruitful place because I will arise and go in the name of the Lord.' And the Lord would commend you. My daughter, I commend you this day. Continue to do what you determine to do in your spirit, and I will meet you on the level of the supernatural. And I will see you through. And you will have a fruitful ministry because you are determined."

"Because you'll not give up."

What exactly did that mean? I wondered.

What was there for me not to give up?

I didn't know. I didn't understand.

But it was clearly a word from the Lord. And it was clear to me that there was something waiting for me that He was already preparing me for.

Mary's Predicament

Mary, the mother of Jesus, received a word from the Lord once and she didn't understand it either. But she also didn't let her lack of understanding get in the way of receiving that word when the angel Gabriel spoke to her. She just sat back and let God be God and do whatever He wanted for her and through her. Luke 1:28-35 records what happened when Mary was visited by the angel of the Lord:

And the angel came in unto her, and said, Hail, thou that art highly favoured, the Lord is with thee: blessed art thou among women. And when she saw him, she was troubled at his saying, and cast in her mind what manner of salutation this should be. And the angel said unto her, Fear not, Mary: for thou hast found favour with God. And, behold, thou shalt conceive in thy womb, and bring forth a son, and shalt call his name JESUS. He shall be great, and shall be called the Son of the Highest: and the Lord God shall give unto him the throne of his father David: And he shall reign over the house of Jacob for ever; and of his kingdom there shall be no end. Then said Mary unto the angel, How shall this be, seeing I know not a man? And the angel answered and said unto her, The Holy Ghost shall come upon thee, and the power of the Highest shall overshadow thee: therefore also that holy thing which shall be born of thee shall be called the Son of God.

The Bible goes on to recount the birth of Jesus, and how an angel of the Lord visited shepherds, told of this miraculous birth, and instructed them as to where they could find the child. When the men went to Bethlehem, found Mary, her husband Joseph, and the baby Jesus, and told of their experience, the Bible says Mary "kept all these things, and pondered them in her heart" (Luke 2:19).

I can imagine the kinds of thoughts Mary had that day. First of all, she had experienced her own visitation from an angel of the Lord, who had told her something that, in the natural, was impossible. Yet there she was, nine months later, with the living proof of what the Lord had said was going to happen to her.

She had a baby boy, and had never slept with a man.

"Because you'll not give up!"

Those words were back. Reverberating inside my head as I wondered what they could possibly mean.

Surely, it would be something good!

I did what Mary did.

I held them close to my heart, and I pondered them. I didn't know what was out there in front of me, but I would have to trust

God. I would have to lean on those words of encouragement for whatever opportunity or challenge lie ahead.

I was encouraged "not to give up."

———— ❧ ————

*P*_{*ray this prayer:*}

Dear Father, I'm learning the importance of patiently waiting on You. Sometimes, it's easy to rush and make rash decisions when everything looks, sounds, and feels just right. More and more I understand why You warn me not to live according to the demands of my physical body and my natural feelings, and why You encourage me to follow Your Holy Spirit within me. He personally teaches me Your Word, helps me remember it, and guides me according to Your Word. And, thank You for men and women whom You choose to teach and speak Your Word by Your Holy Spirit, in Jesus' name. Amen.

Scriptures for Meditation: Genesis 12:1-3; Luke 1:28-35; Psalm 40:1; Proverbs 14:12; Romans 8:1; John 14:26; John 16:13; 1 Peter 1:21

Chapter 6

The Favor of God

The first three years of our marriage were great. Like most newlyweds, we did fun things together. We surprised each other by planning weekend trips, went out to dinner, watched movies. We were in love, and just enjoyed being together!

Most importantly, I wanted God to be the center of our lives and He was. As students, we studied together and we always prayed together. We had also become leaders at the church we attended. Our lives were full as Greg and I were learning the Word of God, how to apply it to our lives, and how to live and walk by faith. We were preparing to be sent out someday to work full-time in some capacity in the ministry.

To look at us, we were the model couple.

Greg was in school full time, so he didn't work a full-time job. I attended Bible school in the morning and worked in the afternoons as a domestic, doing housecleaning for $10 an hour. Though the income was enough to sustain us, I felt it was not God's perfect will for me. The Lord confirmed that for me when I prayed and asked for His direction.

An Open Door

I can't say I was surprised when the Lord answered me so quickly. What was unclear to me, though, was that in my heart I heard Him tell me where to go to work and to become "a floater secretary." I'd never heard of a "floater secretary" before, so you can imagine my shock when I called to inquire about job open-

ings and was told they had a position for a "floater secretary."
The job, which paid $2.50 an hour, required that I "float," serving
anyone who needed a secretary.

I remembered Oral Roberts declaring several years earlier
that "Something good is going to happen to you!" and I believed
it.

A "floater secretary" was not the most stable position, but it
was a job. The important thing was that I felt I was in God's will,
and that He was working to fulfill His plan for my life.

Earlier, when I was praying, I had heard the Lord speak to
my heart: "Remain faithful and I will promote you." That was
confirmed by the fact that my salary began to increase almost
with every paycheck.

God was always faithful to me.

One day, as I read over several postings on the bulletin board,
I saw a certain position available.

I told the Lord, "If this job is for me, work out the details."

Not long after that, I got a call from the personnel office asking me to come in for an interview. As I was leaving the office
following the interview, I sensed God's presence. In my heart, I
heard these words: "You will get this job, and it will be the beginning of your ministry."

Shortly after completing my second year at Bible school, I
went to work full time.

"Because you'll not give up."

The words came rushing back.

Was this what the pastor meant when he gave me those words
of exhortation?

It sure appeared that it was.

There I was, a young girl fresh out of Bible school and already working for and with some honored and respected leaders
in the Christian world.

The Bible says in Proverbs 18:16, "A man's gift maketh room
for him, and bringeth him before great men." At that early stage
of my life as a believer, I wasn't sure what, if any, special gift
the Lord may have given me. I just knew I loved God with all
my heart, and deep down inside me I had such a deep and abid-

ing passion to serve Him in whatever way I could. Nevertheless, whatever it was that God had placed on the inside of me was already working on my behalf. On occasion, executives and leaders would call and ask me to pray with them or I would be asked to provide words of encouragement.

Why me? I wondered. In a way, that I would be singled out and asked to pray reminded me of the story of young Joseph and how he was betrayed by his brothers—first thrown into a pit and left to die, and then retrieved from the pit and literally sold as a slave. In the end, the whole thing worked out for Joseph's good because the Lord was with him.

> And Joseph was brought down to Egypt; and Potiphar, an officer of Pharaoh, captain of the guard, an Egyptian, bought him of the hands of the Ishmaelites, which had brought him down thither. And the LORD was with Joseph, and he was a prosperous man; and he was in the house of his master the Egyptian. And his master saw that the LORD was with him, and that the LORD made all that he did to prosper in his hand. And Joseph found grace in his sight, and he served him: and he made him overseer over his house, and all that he had he put into his hand. And it came to pass from the time that he had made him overseer in his house, and over all that he had, that the LORD blessed the Egyptian's house for Joseph's sake; and the blessing of the LORD was upon all that he had in the house, and in the field (Genesis 39:1-5).

Joseph literally went from obscurity as a slave to overseeing the entire staff in his master's household. Talk about favor! Years later, when he found himself in the presence of his brothers—the very ones who had turned their backs on him—Joseph told them, with a forgiving heart, "Now therefore be not grieved, nor angry with yourselves, that ye sold me hither: for God did send me before you to preserve life ... God sent me before you to preserve you a posterity in the earth, and to save your lives by a great deliverance (Genesis 45:5,7).

There I was, talking with and praying with leaders at my place of employment. Just as it had been spoken to me, the Lord had brought my gift before great men (and women). Truly, God's favor was with me.

The following year, I learned I was pregnant with my second child. Greg was finishing up his second year of Bible school and I was still working full time. I continued to work right up until it was time to have the baby.

I knew I was carrying a boy, and the Lord told me to name him Jason. Before he was born, I would read the Word of God to him out loud and tell him what a mighty man of God he was going to be. My labor lasted only about an hour and Jason made his entrance into the world. I would not be honest if I didn't tell you that almost immediately, I thought about the tragedy that befell me with my firstborn. Fear tried to creep in, but I wouldn't allow it. God had blessed me once again to have this sweet little bundle of joy, and I refused to let the devil rob me, or my husband, of the joy we were experiencing at that moment.

Cradling my baby in my arms, I looked him in the eyes and declared that I was committed to teach and train him to love the Lord. I would see to it, I told him that he would grow to serve God with all his heart, soul, and mind.

Early in his little life, Jason was challenged with jaundice. He also battled with seizures that, at times, were so severe he had to be hospitalized. The last attack came when he was in his pre-school years. Doctors thought he had spinal meningitis, but that was later proven to not be the case. We prayed and God miraculously healed our son. He never suffered another seizure. Jason accepted the Lord when he was almost six years old and was water baptized a year and a half later. I remember his excitement with getting baptized and how he even fasted all that day. He told everybody he could about his experience. It was an exciting day for all of us, and it was great to see his enthusiasm for the Lord.

Being a mother is one of the greatest callings in life. I decided to stay home after Jason was born.

*P*ray this prayer:

Dear Father, I do not understand why there's been such heartache and disappointment in my life. I guess the saying is true that sometimes bad stuff happens to good people. I love You with all my heart, and I choose to trust and believe You no matter what comes and goes. You promise that even though I might face many troubles, yet You're right there with me every time, and You rescue me from each and every one of them. And, according to Your Word, all things work together and are fitting into a plan for my good because I love You.

Scriptures for Meditation: Proverbs 18:16; Genesis 12:1-3, 39:1-5, 45:5, 7; Psalm 34:19; Psalm 91:15 MSG; NASB; Romans 8:28 AMP

Chapter 7

❧

A Double Dose of Failure

*I*t's been said that lightning never strikes twice in the same place. I'd like to meet the person who came up with that revelation because, trust me, I can vouch for the fact that it does. Only with me it felt more like a tsunami.

Greg finished his final year of Bible school and was ordained to preach. Immediately, we began seeking God for direction. We needed to know what He wanted us to do with what we had learned. Greg knew he had been called to pastor and, ironically, believed he was to start a church in a town near where my parents lived. I was less than enthused at the idea than he was. Returning home would not have created a problem for me, but now that God had moved me on to something different, I didn't particularly care to return to the past. But I was committed to being a faithful wife, and I wanted to please Greg in every way possible. If that meant going back home, then I was more than willing.

We moved in with my parents, where we remained just long enough to find a place of our own. Things were moving quickly, and in no time, we were settled into a nice house and planning our first church service.

We had rented an old building to meet for services. But the building was so old, it became very costly to keep it warm in the winter. We decided to move our church meetings to the basement of our home. We quickly outgrew our basement, and started meeting in our garage. Finally, we moved into a building along the highway that was suitable in every way. Attendance grew fast as people drove from all around.

Those early days serving as pastors were fun, but they were also very difficult times. Greg had to get outside work to keep us afloat financially, and I helped him in ministry as best I could. We both enjoyed our lives as pastors.

Or, so I thought.

From Subtle to Openly Obvious

I cannot pinpoint exactly when it started, but I first began to realize something was wrong when I noticed a difference in Greg's preaching. Sermons that had been filled with God's love, joy, and peace were suddenly laced with falsehoods, fabrications and, in some cases, outright lies.

Every Mother's Day, for instance, Greg told the members how much he loved me and rattled off a long laundry list of the things he did for me. The truth is, things were becoming very difficult in our marriage. Rarely did we communicate on any kind of "civil" level, and Greg did hardly anything for me. When I would confront him about his comments, his attitude was always very nonchalant, negative, or defensive. He would say things like, "I didn't say that," or "Just don't tell anybody."

Jason also recognized the lies. He confronted his father about it and Greg told him: "People will never find out. That's our secret."

How do you rationalize lying in the pulpit? As a pastor, how do you rationalize lying at all?

Greg was making things up just to make his sermons sound better and make himself look good before the congregation.

The sad part is that Greg never appeared remorseful regarding his actions.

As time passed, things got progressively worse. Greg was displaying all sorts of odd behavior.

For example, once when he was preaching on child discipline, Greg decided to give the congregation an object lesson. Jason had been sitting quietly beside me on the front row as his father was preaching. Suddenly, Greg stopped preaching and walked over to Jason and took him by the hand. The two of them then went into a back room, where Greg proceeded to spank

Jason. I could hear Jason's cries coming from the back, and so could everyone else. When they returned, Greg continued with his message, never once offering an explanation to a confused and stunned congregation. He later told me it had been a while since Jason had been spanked and it was time.

I had envisioned my home as one filled with peace, love, and contentment. We both did. It was our constant prayer. We both wanted God to be at the center of our marriage, to lead and guide us. Soon, I noticed Greg not praying as often. And he made excuses to not pray with me.

The only time there was peace inside those four walls was when Greg was not around. Much of my time was spent with the Lord and with Jason, watching Christian programming and children's shows. Though we pastored a church, behind the scenes Greg and I had very little in common.

I once heard there is a philosophy that says if you successfully raise a child to the age of six years old, that child will usually live by that same philosophy for the rest of their life. The thought is that whatever ideas and ideologies that go into shaping the character of the child are instilled in the child's mind by the age of six. Whether that is true or not, the Bible teaches that when we are born again we need to renew our minds to the things of God. Old habits and ways are done away with as we are kept by the power of God (2 Corinthians 5:17). If we don't spend the appropriate time with God, allowing Him to keep us from those things through the power of His Holy Spirit, then at some point we are subject to slip back over into that old way of thinking, doing, and acting.

Maybe I didn't want to accept it, but it was obvious that was exactly what was happening to Greg. More and more Greg's character traits, the ones he had before we were married, were beginning to resurface. Day by day, I was witnessing my husband returning to his old lifestyle.

Despite the change I saw in Greg, I was determined to make our marriage work—to be a devoted wife and pray for my husband. I wanted so desperately to be that wise, successful wife that the Bible describes in Proverbs 31. I supported him as a wife, but it takes two willing spouses to make a marriage work. Love pays no attention to a suffered wrong. That's what the Bible says in 1 Corinthians 13:4 (AMP). It was obvious that Jason and I were suffering. I was trying to "fix" the situation by being a "good wife" who quietly endured the abuse when I should have been screaming at the top of my lungs for help.

Greg needed help. He needed counseling. But rather than offer him help, I masked it. I kept our problems secret so that no one would know. One failed marriage was enough. What would my family, friends, or congregation think if they knew this one was in trouble?

I didn't realize that by not acknowledging the problem, I was only feeding it.

Joy Comes In a Bundle

Before we were married, Greg and I had agreed that we would have at least two children. With our marriage so unstable, bringing another child into the picture was the absolute last thing I wanted to do. When I shared my feelings with Greg, he insisted things were better, insisting he had changed and that I could trust him.

Soon after I became pregnant, I discovered Greg was right. He had changed, but not for the better.

I went into labor one evening just as we were set to leave home for church services. Greg took me to the hospital, but it was clear he wasn't happy at the timing of my labor and the fact that it was getting in the way of his being able to preach that evening. When we arrived at the hospital, he was literally yelling and condemning me, demanding that I "get the show on the road." You can imagine my embarrassment I felt, not to mention the shock and surprise on the faces of those at the hospital.

My concern over what Greg might do or say became so strong that my contractions, which had been coming at a steady pace, suddenly slowed and finally stopped completely. The following morning, doctors were forced to induce labor.

I gave birth to a beautiful baby boy, our second bundle of joy. Greg let me name him Joel. As I looked into the face of my precious newborn, I tried to not think of the drama of the last several hours and how my husband, who represented himself to our church congregation and to the community as a man of God, had acted so ungodly and embarrassed us all. Instead, I reflected on God's blessing of that moment, and the special gift He had given us. I rejoiced in my heart that we now had another son. The Bible says in Psalm 30:5, "...weeping may endure for a night, but joy cometh in the morning." The Lord impressed me that this baby was a gift from Him and I would see that in years to come.

Greg's actions on the previous evening had not only brought me shame and disgrace, but on the inside I was hurting. How could someone who professed such a caring and affectionate love for his wife when standing before a congregation, become so selfish and unkind behind closed doors?

I didn't want to admit it, but there was no getting around the obvious. My heart's cry was that I wanted my marriage to work, but it was only getting worse. The verbal abuse I was receiving from my husband was now becoming physical—almost on a daily basis. The handwriting was as clearly etched on the wall as it could be, and I was reading it like I had written it myself. For a second time, my marriage was in trouble. Once again, I was staring failure smack in the face. Soon, I would be faced with the huge challenge of raising two children all by myself.

Pray this prayer:

Dear Father, in obedience to Your Word, I choose to forgive those who are unkind to me—even when they hurt me again and again. I dare not forget the many times—even in one day—that I've come to You to confess and repent of my wrongdoing. I realize that forgiveness is a major part of loving. Your Word also says the way to determine and identify whether a person is good or bad is by their words which come from deep within their heart, and their deeds and lifestyle. Thank You for Your Holy Spirit Who reveals the truth to me, and Your Word which is like a lamp and a light that shows and helps me to know what steps to take and what path to follow to get out of this dark situation, in Jesus' name. Amen.

Scriptures for Meditation: 2 Corinthians 5:17; 1 Corinthians 13:4 AMP; Psalm 30:5; Matthew 18:21-22; Ephesians 4:32; Matthew 12:33-35; Matthew 7:16,20; John 16:13; Psalm 119:105; John 3:21

Chapter 8

Joy Turns to Abuse

Not long ago, I read an article about a couple and their three children who were having dinner at a New Jersey restaurant when the husband suddenly became angry after their waiter disappeared for more than twenty minutes.

First, the husband began muttering to himself, the wife recalled. Then, all of a sudden he yelled out loud across the room to another waiter, "Excuse me!" and stormed off to find the manager.

When the original waiter returned to the table, the husband yelled: "Where the hell have you been for the last forty-five minutes?" He then proceeded to berate the young waiter until the man walked off.

Embarrassed, all the wife could do was lower her head, and cover her eyes. There's no telling what or how her children felt while watching their father experience what society commonly refers to as a "meltdown" right there in the middle of a crowded restaurant.

Asked later how her husband's behavior—which the wife admitted happened on a fairly regular basis—affected her, the woman said she found his habit of loudly confronting waiters, store managers, or noisy people in movie theaters, extremely embarrassing. When she confronted him about it, she said he brushed off her concerns and insisted his behavior was warranted.

Reading that article, I could not help but put my husband in the place of the man at that table. The only difference was that Greg would not have been satisfied with just screaming and yelling.

Greg got angry a lot. When he did, he threw things.

More often than not, his target was usually either Jason or me.

After we were married, Greg's parents told me their son frequently lost his temper. They said at times he got violent.

When I asked him about it, Greg acknowledged he had suffered a bad temper even as far back as his childhood—I guess the old-fashioned word is "tantrum." He even admitted that once he lost his temper and got into a fight that almost landed him in jail.

I never saw that side of him during the short time we dated, but then that's not surprising. You always put your best foot forward when you're trying to impress someone, especially a date or a "love interest," and Greg had done exactly that. But now that we were married, he didn't conceal anything. The real Greg had started to come out, and from all indications, he was making no effort to hide it.

That was not good news for me, Jason, or Joel.

Greg appeared to become angry at the drop of a hat. There was never any warning.

And the abuse seemed constant!

He would do things like lock me and the boys in the bathroom, and keep us there for hours. Other times, he would walk throughout the house, yelling and slamming doors.

Once, he got so upset he threw Jason into some furniture, hurting his ear badly and causing it to bleed. Another time, as he was feeding Joel his bottle, Greg deliberately held the bottle in Joel's mouth until our baby began gasping for air. When I asked him to stop, Greg laughed and said he wanted to see the baby struggle.

What kind of father deliberately tortures his child?

Greg didn't seem to care who witnessed his strange actions either.

One Sunday after church, we were having dinner with some church members when Greg became upset and kicked Joel's baby walker across the floor—with Joel sitting in it.

Greg was rough when he played with Jason. Sometimes, I wondered if his roughness was deliberate and if he was trying to hurt our son. Once, he and Jason were playing too hard and

Jason's collarbone was broken. Greg saw the playing as just fun. But although Jason never said anything to me, I could tell he didn't like the way his daddy played most of the time. My suspicions were confirmed one night when Jason woke up screaming after apparently having a nightmare. In his sleep, he was yelling, "No, Daddy! No, Daddy! Don't hurt me! No! No!"

There were times when Jason and I would not even go outside the house because the bruises from encounters with Greg were so visible. I didn't want to have to explain what had happened and cast my husband in a bad light. After all, he was a preacher. It was very embarrassing when he had those kinds of outbursts. But, it never seemed to bother or embarrass Greg. Most of the time, he pretended he didn't even recall the incident. Other times, when I would bring them up, he denied them and called me a liar.

Once, I watched as Greg tried to pick up my dad and throw him down some stairs. He was violent with other people as well.

My only place of solace was in God's Word. It was through reading my Bible and praying that I found strength to continue—to remain in a relationship that I knew in my heart appeared to be doomed. Jason loved to pray with me. I didn't know it then, but he was going to become my little prayer partner.

Clearly, there appeared something was wrong with my husband—spiritually, mentally, and emotionally. And though he would not admit it, I knew he needed help. We ALL needed help.

A few times, Greg talked about being depressed and said he had contemplated suicide. I didn't know the signs of depression and, quite frankly, I had no reason to believe him. I thought he was just feeling sorry for himself because of the way he acted and treated us, and that he was trying to manipulate me to feel sorry for him. Sometimes, Greg could act as much like a baby as our two sons.

The truth was I needed answers—quickly! This was definitely not the marriage I had dreamed of, and it didn't look as though it would ever be. When I talked with Greg about our marital situation, he showed no interest. What was I to do?

In the natural, I felt all alone. But in my heart, I knew God was with me. I also knew that if I asked for His help, God would help me. He always had. My assurance came through God's Word in Isaiah 26:3-4: "Thou wilt keep *him* in perfect peace, *whose* mind *is* stayed *on thee*: because he trusteth in thee. Trust in the Lord for ever: for in the Lord Jehovah *is* everlasting strength."

Perfect peace?

Our marriage was a long way from resembling perfect peace—in fact, peace, period. And with each passing day, it was getting further and further away. I had to do something—not just for my safety, but for our two sons. But what?

I decided to leave Greg. Not for good. Just long enough to sort things—to figure out what was best for all of us.

Greg worked during the day, so I knew he would be away for several hours. I got Jason and Joel, packed up a few things and left home. Later that evening, I called Greg and told him why I had left. He apologized for his actions, and pleaded with me to return.

Though I told Greg I forgave him, I wondered if I really did. I was still angry, and I was hurt. Hurt that he had deceived me into thinking he was something that he was not. Hurt by the thought that my marriage was not what I had hoped for, nor would it likely ever be. Hurt that the man I loved so dearly had turned into such a monster.

I couldn't go back. At least not right away.

"What will I tell the church?" Greg asked me.

"Tell them anything you want," I said. "You've told so many lies about us already." It was so good to get away and not have the physical and verbal abuse.

Even as we talked, I knew that at some point I would have to go back to my husband and give our marriage another chance to work out.

But I was tired of the abuse, and I wasn't ready to take on any more.

From Bad to Very Bad

Things had been bad before I left Greg.

He promised that if I came back, things would be better.

One of the things Greg complained about often was how frustrated he was over his ministry. Not the growth of the church, but the fact that he had to spend so much time studying and preparing to preach on Sundays and our mid-week service. What was once a passion for him now appeared to be boredom and a burden. I was as confused as he was frustrated. He never said so, but I often felt that Greg wasn't happy with himself and how he had turned out as a minister. From his first year in Bible school, he had sensed God's call on his life to pastor. All he had faced since entering the ministry was hardship. His church was growing, but he told me he didn't know how to handle the church challenges or our marriage, including being the kind of husband, father, and provider he knew God required him to be.

Greg, I believe, was still being haunted by those things when I finally decided to return home. I suggested we move to another location and give our marriage a fresh start, but he said no.

In essence, nothing had changed.

We had just returned home from church one Sunday afternoon when Greg brought up his frustrations again. He talked about a "time bomb" inside him that could go off at any moment. Then he said the unimaginable:

"I'm going to kill my family and then turn the gun and kill myself."

My first thought was to run—to grab my boys and get away just as fast as I could. But I was too shocked to move. So instead, I listened as Greg explained that killing us all would bring an end to his frustrations.

A few days passed without incident.

Then, it happened!

My parents decided to move south for the winter, and I asked if Jason could visit with them for a few days before they left.

After a couple of days of not noticing that his son was missing, Greg asked me where Jason was. When I explained that he was visiting with his grandparents for a few days, Greg became angry that he had not been consulted. I tried explaining that Jason would only be gone for one day, but he got even more upset that I didn't discuss the matter with him in advance.

Greg went into a closet and took out his high-powered rifle, then looked at me and said, "I'm going to bring him home, dead or alive." He then left the house in a rage.

Shocked and frightened, I watched as Greg angrily stormed out of the house and got into the car. I had seen him angry before, but never to this degree. And considering what he had said two days earlier, I thought it was extremely possible that he would follow through with his threat to kill us all.

For the next hour or so, I watched out the window as Greg sat in the car, still parked in the driveway. Joel remained sound asleep in his crib.

When I saw Greg getting out of the car and heading for the house, I hid behind the sofa. Still very angry, Greg yelled out to me, but I didn't answer.

"Okay, I'll put the gun up!" he said.

When I came out of hiding, Greg held me at gunpoint in the kitchen, and cocked the lever and said he was going to kill me. He was furious and out of control. My heart was racing. He was determined to take my life that day. I could see it in his eyes. But the Lord had a different plan. I cried out to God and began quoting Scripture to myself, personalizing each of them.

"My angels are encamped around about me to keep me safe from all harm" — (Psalm 34:7).

"God hath not given me the spirit of fear, but of power, and of love, and of a sound mind" — (2 Timothy 1:7).

"No weapon formed against me shall prosper" — (Isaiah 54:17).

"Greater is He that is in me, then he that is in the world" — (1 John 4:4).

"I overcome by the blood of the Lamb and the word of my testimony" — (Revelation 12:11).

"I will live and not die! I plead the blood of Jesus over me."

Slowly, Greg lowered the gun. Then, just as quickly as he had rushed into the house, he retreated and ran outside. Shaken, I felt my legs trembling. I recall very little of the remainder of that day, other than the fact that Greg eventually returned home and said nothing about what had happened.

That night, I slept in Jason's bedroom.

Last Ditch Effort

Up to that point, I had not truly confided in my parents about all my marital problems. Though they were not the kind of parents who meddled in my marriage, I'm sure they knew things were not good.

The next morning, after Greg left for work, I called and told them what happened. My father became extremely upset and insisted I report the incident to local authorities. Taking his advice, I had someone watch Joel while I went to the authorities to file a complaint.

Rather than look into the incident, or talk with Greg, they suggested I have him committed to a mental institution. Instead, I talked with Greg and suggested we consider getting some help through marriage counseling. You can imagine my surprise when my husband agreed.

I called and made an appointment to meet with a Christian marriage counselor. I was excited that, finally, we were going to get the help we needed, and I could only hope Greg was just as excited. Much to my disappointment, the day we went for our first counseling session, the counselor informed us that he and his wife were no longer together.

After that failed attempt to save our marriage, things got even worse.

More and more, Greg began to distance himself from the boys and me. Often, he would leave home early in the mornings and not return until after midnight. Sometimes, he wouldn't return until three or four the next morning. When I asked why he was leaving so early and staying out most of the night, he refused to answer. Greg also began showing signs of resentment toward me and my determination to read the Bible and pray.

One day a lady called to tell Greg how encouraged she was after I had taken the time to talk with her and share Scripture. After speaking with the woman, Greg hung up the phone, looked at me and told me to never do that again or he would hurt me. What had I done that was so wrong? I wondered. As pastors, it was our responsibility to share God's Word and offer encouragement to those who needed it. I thought, *This is crazy!*

I knew the day would come when I would leave Greg for good. I had tried everything I knew to save our marriage, and nothing had worked. We talked more about the incident, then Greg, still demanding I not counsel people, delivered to me the ultimate of ultimatums: "Either choose God or me."

It was another one of those "out of nowhere" moments.

At first, I couldn't believe he would say such a thing. A pastor, one who is solely committed to the saving of souls, not only insisting his wife not share God's Word, but also telling her to stop reading the Bible! It was unthinkable, but true.

I loved God's Word. It was, and still is, my life. It's my strength. Take the Word from me and you may as well take away my life.

Greg may have expected me to cave in at his unreasonable demand—out of fear, if for no other reason. But that wasn't about to happen. It wasn't a difficult decision to make. And although I didn't respond right away, I already knew what my answer would be.

After that, I lost my desire to go to church with Greg. I began making up excuses to stay home. As much as I thought I loved him, I didn't want to be around him anymore. He represented everything that was contrary to what I believed a man of God should be—what I wanted MY man of God to be.

I couldn't believe I was thinking it, but yes, more and more I wanted out of our marriage. I never gave voice to those thoughts, but I may as well have come right out and told God how I felt. He knew anyway.

One day as I was praying, I heard the Lord say to me, "Are

you willing to go and leave all your things behind?" To be honest, the question caught me off guard. What exactly did He mean, "…leave all your things behind"? I didn't immediately respond to the Lord either. Instead, I offered to get back with Him. I know, it does sound crazy. But, I really don't think God was bothered by my reaction. It wasn't the first time someone hesitated or refused to answer or respond to His profound questions.

In the Book of Luke, Jesus told a story about a wealthy young man who, though he had everything imaginable, wanted to know how he could inherit eternal life. Here's how his conversation with Jesus went:

> And a certain ruler asked him, saying, Good Master, what shall I do to inherit eternal life? And Jesus said unto him, Why callest thou me good? none is good, save one, that is, God. Thou knowest the commandments, Do not commit adultery, Do not kill, Do not steal, Do not bear false witness, Honour thy father and thy mother. And he said, All these have I kept from my youth up. Now when Jesus heard these things, he said unto him, Yet lackest thou one thing: sell all that thou hast, and distribute unto the poor, and thou shalt have treasure in heaven: and come, follow me. And when he heard this, he was very sorrowful: for he was very rich (Luke 18:18-23).

No doubt, this rich man wasn't expecting the response he got from Jesus. Well, neither was I expecting to hear those words, "Leave all your things behind," as I prayed early that morning. Practically all our possessions and furnishings were either things I brought into our marriage, or antiques that had been given to us. I had paid for most of them. But it didn't take me long to realize I really had no choice. God wasn't giving me an option. He was showing me the way out—the way to escape. I had ignored all the warning signs before, but I wasn't about to overlook this one.

"Because you'll not give up."

Those words from that pastor were hidden in my heart.

Does leaving everything behind mean that I'm finally giving up? I wondered.

No, I reasoned. It simply means I'm finally ready to move on. Possessions were nice, but they didn't have a hold on me. I needed to be safe. My sons needed to be safe. God heard my cry, and had come to our rescue. Our marriage was in serious trouble. In fact, this wasn't even a marriage. We just happened to live in the same house and had the same last name.

My mind was made up. I said out loud, "Lord, I'm ready to leave everything behind!"

———— ∞ ————

*P*ray *this prayer:*

Dear Father, You promise to watch over me and to hear my prayers, even before I finish praying. So, even when it seems that the more I pray, the worse my situation becomes, I yet continue to believe and trust You. With all my heart, I love You and I believe You love me. You're good to me and You have nothing but my best interests at heart. The emotional hurt and pain are harder to bear than the physical abuse. This burden is too heavy for me so, please help me to cast the care of all my hurts into Your hands, just like I have entrusted You with my life. Thank You for completely healing me. I am asking You for the joy and strength to keep looking up to You for help to recover and not give up, in Jesus' name. Amen.

Scriptures for Meditation: Isaiah 26:3-4; Luke 18:18-23; 1 Peter 3:12; Isaiah 65:24; Isaiah 26:3-4; 1 Peter 5:7; Nehemiah 8:10; Psalm 121:2

Chapter 9

❦

Our Flight for Freedom

By now, my parents were well aware of the problems Greg and I were having. Never ones to interfere, they had expressed their concerns to me only, and had supported me in the best way they knew how—through prayer. But my father had made it clear that if things ever got seriously out of hand, or if I thought our lives were in danger, then I should take the boys and leave.

Dad kept a second car in the garage of his home as a spare, and had told me that if I ever needed it, the gas tank was full and there was $50 in the glove box.

That time had finally come.

My mother would sometimes call the house to check on my boys and me. When she did, most times she wouldn't say anything. She just stayed on the line in silence, waiting for me to speak.

'This Is the Day!'

It was a Friday in March. As he did every weekday morning, Greg left home early to go to work. I had been spending time with the Lord, reading my Bible and praying, when the phone rang.

Greg had mentioned sometime back that he suspected our phones were bugged. I thought it was just another one of his wild illusions, but still I was careful in what I said when I talked on the phone.

This time, I picked up the receiver but said nothing. There was silence on the other end as well, which led me to believe it was my mom. After a few moments, I broke the silence by quoting a verse from Psalm 118:24. Speaking softly, I said: "This *is* the day *which* the Lord hath made; we will rejoice and be glad in it." Then I hung up the phone. If it was my mom on the other end, I knew she would understand that scripture as code that meant I was preparing to leave Greg that day. Besides, I had previously written my parents that I would be leaving my husband because of all the abuse, but I just didn't know when.

While Greg was gone, I spent most of the day putting a few things in each of the several closets in the house so they would be easy to get to and move quickly to the car when the time was right. I had rehearsed my packing routine over and over in my head, so I knew it would not be a difficult process. I just needed to make sure Greg would be away from the house long enough for me to get everything packed.

In addition to serving as pastor of the church, Greg was also pastor of the Singles' ministry. I later learned that, although he conducted counseling sessions, Greg was also visiting with some of the single women, one-on-one, in their homes. I didn't have to wonder what was taking place during those "counseling sessions." What wasn't already obvious to me was confirmed in conversations I later had with some of those women.

Before Greg left for church that evening, I removed Joel's car seat from our "good" car. When he was gone, I began loading up the spare car with the belongings I had been secretly placing in the closets. Most of what I packed was for the boys, including a playpen, high chair, stroller, and walker. But I was careful to take along some things for myself as well, especially a pretty dress and some jewelry.

I wish I could say I had a bit of remorse about what I was doing, but I didn't. In truth, I was happy. I never wanted my marriage to end. I loved my husband and I thought he loved me. But that had been proven not to be the case long ago. Now, I was doing the only reasonable thing possible. I was fleeing for the safety and lives of my two children and myself.

It was my decision. No one had coerced me into leaving Greg. In fact, I don't believe anyone can ever truly talk you into leaving your spouse. That's a decision you have to make for yourself. And you must make it for all the right reasons.

In my case, my children and I had become the victims of horrendous abuse—both mental and physical. If we were to survive, then we needed to escape. And the Lord had seen to it that we could do just that. I had had enough, and now I was determined to not allow them and myself to take it any more. God always makes a way to escape.

By now, it was 8 o'clock. The phone was ringing.

Should I answer it, or should I just keep packing? I wondered.

I picked up the phone, but there was silence on the other end. My mother was calling again.

Standing still, I spoke softly a single word: "Soon."

Then, I hung up.

Out of obedience to the Lord, I left my possessions behind and escaped with my small children. They both were under the age of five years old. My youngest was just an infant.

It's funny how, right in the middle of some of the most trying situations, God will throw in a little humor just to ease the tension. I don't know if much of my tension was eased that evening, but the fact that the roads were covered with snow and ice and temperatures had dipped down to around 30 degrees sure did take my mind off of what was really going on for a moment.

The old car I was driving had transmission problems, the tires were balding and the brakes were bad. To this day, I don't know how I managed to maneuver that car the few miles to my parents' house, but I did with God's help.

The plan was to stop at my parents' house, where I would drop off my car and take the one my dad had left behind in case of an emergency.

An Angel Waiting in the Wings

After arriving at my parents' house, I took the boys inside and headed back outside to transfer our things from one car to the other. Beforehand, I phoned my parents to let them know where we were, that we were fine, and that we were about to switch vehicles. They asked me to call them later that night and let them know where we were.

A few weeks earlier I met Jack, one of my parents' neighbors. Knowing that my parents were away, Jack had graciously offered his assistance if I ever needed anything. Fortunately, Jack was at home when I called. I asked him if he would come over and break up the ice and snow that was blocking the garage door so I could get my dad's car out.

In no time at all, Jack had come over. He brought a pick axe with him and went right to work chopping away the ice and frozen snow the winter storm had left behind. Then, he helped me transfer our things from my car to my dad's car. Jack hardly said a word during the transfer. It was as though he knew we were literally running for our lives.

I felt that my husband might come looking for me and knew I had to hurry and get out of there. By now it was almost 10 o'clock and he was likely at home and had discovered that we were gone. My heart was pounding.

Jack had been a godsend. He was truly our "angel waiting in the wings."

I thanked Jack for his help, loaded the boys into the car, and pulled back out on the cold, icy road, headed to the safety and comfort of my parents' presence.

Although it was freezing cold outside, a warm rush of adrenaline flowed through my body. Anxiety had been overcome with joy. For the first time in a very long time, I felt safe. That day in March had become a special day in our lives. We were escaping with only a few possessions.

Driving down the road, I rejoiced and gave praise to God as I thought on His Word in Proverbs 1:33: "Whoever listens to Me will dwell safely, and will be secure, without fear of evil" (personalized).

Our day of deliverance had finally come. Our day of escape!

The further I drove, the sleepier I became. Knowing I was approaching a town large enough to have a motel, I felt assured that

I could at least make it that far. But when I got to the outskirts of that town, I heard a whisper in my head: "Don't stop, keep going." By this time, it was well after midnight. I felt it was the Lord leading me, so I didn't stop. Sometime later, I was prompted to turn down a certain road. A short distance off the highway, was a motel. I checked into the motel, got the kids settled, and then placed the collect call to my parents to let them know where I was. It was 1:30 in the morning.

I later learned that Greg had, in fact, contacted the local sheriff's office when he returned home and found us gone and that he and a sheriff's deputy had begun searching for us. They had gone to my parents' house, where they found the car I'd left behind. Figuring I was likely headed to my parents' home, and assuming I would have to stop at some point so we could rest, they went to the one motel where they thought I would stay for the night. But I had decided to keep going. Fortunately, I had listened to the voice of the Lord and, after driving for an extended period, chose to stop at another motel off the main highway.

We left the motel the next morning, and later we finally arrived in the place where my parents lived. I had called my parents to let them know when to expect us.

Tears flooded my face as we happened to meet my dad at an intersection close to their house. We both pulled off to the side of the road, got out of our cars and embraced. We both cried.

For him, I believe it was just the joy and peace of knowing that his daughter and grandkids were safe. For me, it was a combination of things. I was relieved and happy. I was also extremely exhausted!

Now, we were safe.

Over the next few days, I spent time with God—seeking His direction as to what He wanted me to do next. We had nothing more than the clothes on our backs and the few things I packed for the trip. But for some reason I wasn't worried. There was a peace that filled me that I couldn't explain. To this day, I still cannot explain it. The Lord had done a miraculous work in our lives. He rescued us from a dangerous situation and delivered us safely into the hands of family who loved and cared for us. And

He didn't stop there.

In obedience to Him, I had given it all up. I had walked away from a beautiful home filled with lovely furnishings and antiques. And I had left what friends I had behind. But none of that mattered. We had God's love and protection. And we had each other. In my heart, I knew the Lord would restore what the enemy had stolen. He would give my children and me our lives back.

There was no reason for worry.

———————— ✳✳✳ ————————

*P**ray this prayer:*

Dear Father, I know I can trust You to keep me safe and protected, and to deliver me from all hurt, harm, and danger because Your Word says so. I'm grateful for those who are so compassionate and readily avail themselves to help me when I call them, but they can only go so far, and their resources are limited. However, I run to You to hide and cover me from my enemies and from those who hate me, and to save my life. I am asking You for the courage to do whatever You tell me. Thank You for showing me the way of escape which You have prepared for me, in Jesus' name. Amen.

Scriptures for Meditation: Psalm 118:24; Psalm 91:14; Luke 1:71; Philippians 4:13; 1 Corinthians 10:13

Chapter 10

The Next Step

Three months after I left Greg, I was attending a church service when a man I had never met, and who knew nothing about my situation, spoke prophetically to me some things only the Lord could have revealed to him. Here's what he said:

> "Don't give up hope. Let hope prevail and keep pressing—keep pressing toward hope. I see the gift of intercession, of intercessory prayer and a gift of faith that God is going to release in your heart. We will pray and release those gifts of ministry upon your life. You begin to intercede about that and don't be worried about it. Is this right? Is this the one? Is this what it is supposed to be? … When Moses led the children out of Egypt, they could of gone a way that would have been a shortcut to Canaan Land. But the Lord chose to take them through the wilderness area. We don't know why the Lord has chosen to take you this way. But one thing we are confident, that God is in control of your life, because you have given your life to the Lord. And the Lord is taking you this way for a purpose. There is a purpose that you are going this way.

> "…As you begin to intercede and you begin to pray…the joy of the Lord is going to be renewed in your spirit…it is going to begin to apply pressure to that situation. It is

going to begin to apply pressure to that man. He is going to do one of two things. He is going to obey and turn or he is going to rebel and run. And you are not going to have to ask God, 'Is this or is it not?'

"God is saying, 'Don't look here. Don't look there or look for another one...Believe right where you are. Stand right where you are. Face the battle right where you are, and let the Lord be your vengeance. Let the Lord be your victory.'

"Remain faithful to the Lord and allow the Lord to renew the joy of the Lord and it will renew your strength. And that spirit of intercession is going to come upon you and it is going to apply pressure to the situation and it is going to reveal its motive. It's going to reveal purpose and it's going to reveal its sincerity, its honesty. It's going to reveal it's everything, and then it either will turn under that pressure or it will stand. If it stands, then go after it. If it runs, then leave it."

Those words gave me the encouragement I needed to continue to stand, and not give up hope. I didn't know what God had in store for me and my two sons, but I knew it was something good. Restoration always means something better, and that's where I found myself—in a place of restoration.

I remembered the words of Brother Roberts: "Something GOOD is going to happen to you." I still clung to those words. I was encouraged not to give up hope.

After he learned where we were, Greg wrote letters saying how much he loved me, that he missed me and wanted me to come home. Come home to what? More abuse? If I understood any part of what he was saying, it was that he really did miss having me and the boys around. With us gone, he had no one around to take out his frustrations on. I certainly couldn't understand how he could even believe I would be willing to return to such an abusive situation.

He would have to have changed dramatically, and I had no reason to believe that he had.

Greg came to visit us after we had been gone about three months. I was advised by members of the church we attended not to meet with him alone, and to meet in a public place. My dad went along with the boys and me.

Greg showed little attention to the boys. He seemed more focused on trying to convince me to return home. He even brought along the photo album with our wedding pictures and wanted me to look at them with him. I told him not only was I not interested in looking at the pictures, I really was not happy that he had come to visit.

Not surprising, through all his begging and pleading for me to come back, Greg never once acknowledged he had done anything wrong or asked for forgiveness.

I told him I would not come back.

Shortly after, my parents decided to relocate to another state. My boys and I went with them.

When I told Greg we were moving, and that I would send him the new address when we got settled, he responded: "That's not necessary."

So, did he not care or what?

I should have been surprised at his response, but in reality, I wasn't. Greg had never shown much interest in me or the boys when we were together, so why should he be interested now? Besides, from the reports I was receiving from people I knew when Greg and I were together, he had pretty much moved on with his life in some ways. He had apparently moved out of the house we once shared. It was later confirmed what I had already suspected—that Greg was having an affair with a married woman.

Despite his attitude, I made sure Greg knew where we were and how to contact us.

*P**ray this prayer:*

Dear Father, I know that You are right at hand, and Your presence is all around me like an invisible wall. I am confident in You and I am not afraid. Thank You for the courage, strength, and peace to stand face to face with my enemy at the right time. I am not deceived, swayed, or shaken by what they say, and neither am I intimidated by the looks on their faces. No longer am I an abused victim, in Jesus' name. Amen.

Scriptures for Meditation: Psalm 16:8; Psalm 125:2; Isaiah 41:10; Psalm 27:3; Psalm 89:22; Jeremiah 1:8; Ezekiel 34:22, NLT

Chapter 11

Separate, but Not Apart!

While we were still together, Greg had taken a course on divorce at a nearby community college. I remember him telling me once that a person stood a much better chance at winning in a divorce case if they were the one who filed for the divorce first. It was information that was good to know, but I never thought I'd need it. My husband had already divorced me in his heart. We no longer had a marriage.

The paperwork was bad enough; however, the process itself added to the nightmare. There were challenges at every turn, beginning with the fact that the law required that divorce papers be filed in the state in which we lived as a couple. That meant I would have to travel a long distance back and forth whenever I was needed to appear for a hearing.

I was given temporary custody of both children, but later that fall Greg was granted limited visitation rights. The judge ruled that, because of his history of violence, Greg's visits had to be supervised in my parents' home and Jason and Joel could not stay with him overnight.

Greg traveled to visit with Jason and Joel only twice. Both times, they were resistant toward spending time with him.

A year had passed, and the divorce was not yet final. On occasion, when I would speak with people who knew both Greg and me, and were familiar with our situation, they would describe Greg in such terms as "having mental problems," "not congenial," "very cynical," "dogmatic," and "dangerous and confused." They said he would rationalize his behavior after doing something wrong, and then immediately deny doing it.

One person described him as a "dangerous and unstable man," and warned that I should "do whatever it takes to protect yourself and the children."

The first time we were ready to go to court, the judge assigned to our case died suddenly. When it was discovered that Greg had hired my attorney's brother to represent him, my attorney withdrew from the case, citing a conflict of interest. After having a second attorney refuse to take my case because it was "complicated," I finally hired an experienced lawyer who was a former judge. My financial situation then was very bleak. I wasn't working and was receiving food stamps, and Greg had fallen way behind on his child support payments.

Thankfully, the lawyer took my case without requiring me to pay a retainer fee.

In the meantime, Greg phoned my brother to ask his help in moving my belongings from our house to my parents' home. Praise the Lord! My furniture and things were out of the control of my husband. I was getting it all back. God is so good to me!

My new attorney told me that he would eventually need a retainer fee and asked when I could send the money. My parents decided to have a moving sale and went back to prepare for it. I remained at home with my children.

I told my attorney that my furniture and things were being sold, and that I would send him the money from the proceeds as soon as possible. Thankfully, the money from the sale of all my things was just the right amount to cover the retainer fee, and I quickly mailed off the money to my attorney. Miracles like that just kept happening for us.

The day before our court date, we arrived at my brother and sister-in-law's home. Some friends of ours were there, along with my parents. What a time of prayer and fellowship we had. I slept very well that night. The next morning, I didn't eat breakfast as I felt I needed to pray and meditate on the Word instead. This was going to be our Victory Day!

We drove to the courthouse and I climbed the steps to meet my attorney. He took me into a private room where he went over last minute items and discussed court procedures.

There I was, inside a courthouse and about to begin proceedings to end what possibly had been the worst nightmare imaginable for me and my children.

I was encouraged by my attorney to know my facts, and especially the timetable regarding certain events.

"When they cross examine you," he told me, "don't be rattled. Listen carefully to their questions and don't volunteer any information. Don't use the words, never or always. They may want you to hurry with an answer, but take your time. While you are on the stand and they are asking you questions, look into their eyes. Do the same with the judge. You have nothing to hide. Everything has to be in the best interest of the children."

We entered the courtroom and took our seats. Finally, it was time and the bailiff called out, "Everyone rise!" I took a deep breath. Our future was about to be decided.

"Lord, help me. I need Your favor!"

We spent most of the day in court. Surprisingly, it was nothing like what you see on television. Somehow, you don't feel the tension and stress you experience while watching courtroom drama on TV.

At one point, I leaned over and whispered to my attorney, "It doesn't seem like things are going too well for us!" At that, he whispered back: "You just wait. It is about to bust loose in this courtroom."

Sure enough, things started to happen when my attorney began to cross examine Greg. My attorney, Greg's attorney, and the judge all caught Greg lying. When Greg tried to prove that I was a bad mother, even those summoned to witness on his behalf testified that that was not true.

About a month and a half after our court appearance, we finally received the court decree and our divorce became final. But the nightmare that had plagued us for years was far from over.

The court granted Greg and me joint custody of the children, but ordered that they live with me. Greg was allowed two weeks of visitation during the summer, and was told he could have the boys for another two weeks at some point during the summer if he wanted. This was a major victory, because from what I was told, judges would give the other party up to six or eight week's visitation in the summer.

Greg took advantage of his first two weeks, but that was all. Instead of asking for them again later that summer, he moved. He also didn't take advantage of all his court-assigned visitations.

By this time, we had already had several court sessions. But there would be *many* more—and in three different states.

The following summer, my parents and I decided we would attend a Christian conference in the state where Greg said he lived. He had even given me an address. As part of the court decree, whenever I came within fifty miles of where Greg lived, I was required to contact him so he could see the boys. We looked up Greg at the address he had given me. To our surprise, the address was only to a mailbox store.

I had to get another attorney; this time in the new state where we were living.

When we returned home, God impressed me to believe for full custody of Jason and Joel. I had never heard of a case where the mother was given full custody of her children. I just had to believe God.

As part of the next court orders, Greg was to continue paying child support. However, he didn't make most of the payments.

Greg was also granted phone visitation one night a week. When he did call to talk with the boys, he would wait until 10 or 11 o'clock at night—long after they had gone to bed. When I refused to wake them, Greg became angry and was verbally abusive.

Time Doesn't Heal All Wounds!

They say time heals all wounds.

Not always. At least, not in my case.

It had been more than a year now since Greg and I separated, and finally divorced. Still, I had my moments. There were times when I longed to have my family back—but not like it used to be. And I'm sure my sons did, too. But what I longed for more than anything was to have our lives be safe, stable, and happy and especially to provide a protective and peaceful covering and environment for Jason and Joel.

I wanted that. They needed that!

That would be settled, I hoped, when the court granted me full custody of our sons. I prayed that would happen, and that it would happen soon. I wouldn't give up until it did.

Meanwhile, though we were hundreds of miles apart, Greg continued to cause trouble. Even though he was inconsistent in his child support payments, he demanded that I make the boys available to him according to the designated court visitations. He threatened that if I didn't do as he said, he would take me back to court.

I did my best to comply with the court's instructions, though, at times, I was reluctant to hand the boys over to him. He still showed too many signs of being unstable, and I was very concerned that he might snap at some point and hurt them.

It turned out that I was right.

At Thanksgiving, Greg and I had agreed to meet in a shopping center parking lot so that he could have the boys for the holiday. Knowing how quickly Greg became angry, I had asked two men from our church to accompany us just to be safe. As I got out of the car, Greg walked up and struck me.

"Don't hit me," I pleaded.

"If I hit you again, you will never get up," he said.

In that same meeting, Greg was abusive to the boys, cursing at them and throwing things. When I asked him not to do that, he said, "I can do anything I want to these boys. They are my boys!"

Jason and Joel were both crying, and begging me not to let them go with their daddy. But I had no recourse. I had to obey the court's order, or I would be in trouble.

My heart hurt to see them ride off with Greg.

At times like this, the joy of the Lord had to be my strength. If I didn't have joy, sadness would take me down. Crying and begging God never accomplishes anything. I had to believe that my prayers were effective and I had to trust the Lord. In the natural, there was nothing I could do but lean on Him. Greg drove off with our children, and he was not thinking or acting rationally.

A Trip to Jail—for Me!

Greg was to have the boys back home by 7 o'clock the following Sunday. He arrived forty-five minutes late, offering no excuse. After making several trips to the car to bring in the boys' belongings, Greg hugged Jason and said good-bye, then said he was going back to Jason's bedroom.

"No, leave now," I demanded.

Because I didn't trust him, I had decided never to be alone with my ex-husband. I had asked my Dad to be at the house in case I needed him. Unbeknownst to Greg, Dad was hiding in the kitchen and witnessed what happened next.

Greg grabbed me by the arms and began pushing me toward Jason's bedroom. The force and power of his tight grip made it difficult for me to resist, so I decided not to struggle. Fearful of what he might do, I yelled out, "Call the police!" When he realized my dad was in the house, immediately Greg let me go and ran outside the house. I locked the door behind him, but no sooner than he was outside Greg turned and kicked in the front door. When the police arrived, I showed them the damage to the door, and told them what happened. The police arrested Greg, but when he lied and told them that I was trying to hurt him they also placed me under arrest, put me in handcuffs, and took me to jail.

After placing me in a holding cell and later questioning me, the police determined I had done nothing wrong and let me go. They said that they could see Greg was a violent and angry person, and proceeded to tell me what I should do to stay within the law to protect myself and my children.

"Never swing at him," they advised. "Do everything you can to not make him angry. Don't yell at him, and stay inside your house when he arrives." Because of Greg's previous acts of violence, a restraining order was issued prohibiting him from entering our house.

After that Thanksgiving visitation, Jason made a startling comment:

"Daddy wants to kill you, Mommy," he said to me. "And

he's told me how he is going to do it. He is going to take a knife, stab you and kill you. If he does, how am I going to raise Joel if something happens to you?"

Shocked that Greg would ever say something like that to our son, I reassured Jason that everything was all right—that we would trust God to protect us and that nothing bad would ever happen.

Lord, how much more of this can my children and I take?

Pray this prayer:

Dear Father, thank You for supplying whatever I need day by day. Thank You for Your grace that gives me favor with Yourself and with others so that they favor my just cause by helping and supporting me through this ordeal. I admit that sometimes, I feel helpless and without hope as I face these challenges, but my heart is glad because You love me, help me, and save me, and You make my enemy fail, in Jesus' name. Amen!

Scriptures for Meditation: Philippians 4:19; Luke 1:30; Psalm 35:27; Psalm 109:22,26,28, CEV

Chapter 12

❦

'He Put the Gun Right in My Neck'

*I*t's every mother's nightmare to hear her daughter say that her father has sexually molested her. While the thought is unimaginable, the truth is that kind of abuse goes on every day. And most often, it is not reported or revealed until years later, after the innocent victims have been emotionally and physically wounded and scarred—often beyond healing.

Imagine my horror upon learning not only had my ex-husband put a gun to my young son's head and threatened to kill him, but that he had actually pulled the trigger. Thank God the gun misfired!

This happened one day during the summer, when Jason was about to turn eight years old. Joel had been running a fever that day and, though it was Greg's scheduled time for a court-ordered two-week visitation, I was extremely concerned that Joel did not need to be with his father because he was so sick. Despite my hesitation, I allowed the boys to go with their dad, but I spent much time praying for them and for their safety.

Greg was to have returned the boys home by 6 o'clock on a Sunday night. When the time came and passed, I became concerned and began calling to find out where the three of them were. I became even more concerned when a recording came on at the number Greg had given me saying the phone had been disconnected. Greg had threatened several times before that he was going to take the children and never return them to me.

God, please don't let this be what's happening.

Panic tried to take over my thoughts, but I kept my trust in the Lord and prayed. I refused to fear. I didn't know where my children were, or what was happening. But God knew, and He would protect them. Others joined me in praying for their safety and that they would soon return.

Later that evening, Greg showed up. He offered no excuse for being late.

The next morning, Jason told me, "Mommy, I don't ever want to see my dad again. I don't want any presents from him. I do not want to talk to him on the phone. And I don't want to go by my dad's last name." I didn't pressure him to tell me what happened during the time he and Joel were with their father. A few months later, I wished that I had when Jason came to me and asked, "Can I tell you what happened the last time I saw Daddy?"

In his own words, here's what Jason said took place:

"Daddy was taking Joel and me on a trip. I had been crying and I told him I wanted to go home. 'Please take us home. I want to be with my mom.' Daddy told me to shut up and stop crying, but I just couldn't.

"Because I didn't stop crying, he slammed on the brakes and pulled off the highway. He stopped so fast, I thought we might be going into the ditch. I couldn't think why we had to stop so fast. He went to the back of the van, got out a gun, and opened my door. He put the gun right in my neck. He told me, 'If you don't quit crying, I am going to kill you!' With the gun pointed at my neck, he pulled the trigger but the gun didn't go off. Daddy tried to fix the gun. I could tell he was very angry. He pointed it toward the field and the gun went off. Daddy again pointed the gun toward my neck. He said, 'Now, it will work.' He pulled the trigger and again nothing happened.

"Mommy, I closed my eyes and held my breath and said, 'Jesus.' I said 'Jesus' to myself over and over. Daddy was so mad. He finally put the gun in the back of the van and we drove off down the road. I was still crying. He told me

if I ever told anybody, he was going to kill me for sure.
Joel was in his car seat sound asleep."

By the time he finished telling his story, Jason was crying un-
controllably. I tried to console him, but just recalling the incident
made him so frightened.

I knew something was wrong with Greg, but I never imagined he was in such bad mental or emotional condition as to do
something like that. I knew I needed to do something quickly!
Trembling on the inside, I reminded myself that, no matter what,
I had to stand firm in my faith that God would deliver us from
this terrible situation—that I needed to be strong. I had convinced
myself that this would all be over soon. But in truth, it just kept
getting worse.

I kept speaking the Word of God over our situation, confess-
ing that soon Greg would be out of our lives and that I would
have full custody of my sons. It seemed a lonely and desperate
situation I found myself in, but that didn't matter. I felt the responsibility of my helpless sons whose lives depended upon me,
their mother, to stand in the gap and fight for them.

I told only a few people about our situation, thinking the less
said about it the less I would have to deal with others' opinions
and advice about how to deal with it. Honestly, I didn't need
other people's opinions and advice. I needed their prayers. I
didn't even approach Greg about it, though I wanted desperately
to confront him. I knew he would lie and say it never happened,
just like he lied about a lot of things.

It was later confirmed Jason had told the truth when Greg
asked my brother why Jason would not talk to him.

"It's because of what you have done to him in the past," my
brother answered. Greg responded by saying, "You mean the gun
incident? An eight year old could never remember if a gun was
pulled on him or not."

My brother never mentioned anything about the gun incident
prior to Greg making that comment.

The truth is, my eight year old son did remember the incident. And whether Greg realized it or not, it had left a deeply em-

bedded scar on him. It wasn't long after that incident that Jason began having nightmares—waking up in the middle of the night screaming at his daddy, "Leave me alone!"

A few years later, Jason told me about another incident that happened when Greg took him and Joel along on a camping trip. Jason said Greg tied him and his brother to a tree, in the heat of a blistering sun, while he went off with some of his buddies. Jason said a couple happened by, saw them tied to the tree, and let them loose.

After hearing that story, there was no question as to what needed to happen. Suddenly, this entire episode had turned into a life or death situation for Jason and Joel. It was no longer just about me. It was about their safety and lives as well, and I was responsible to make sure no harm would come to them. Greg must no longer be anywhere near myself or my sons.

---

*P*ray this prayer:

Dear Father, there seems to be no end to the hatred and violent threats of my enemy. Thank You for Your presence that goes with me, and comforts me on every side. No matter how large and strong my enemy appears to be, and how small and weak I may feel, I trust Your Word that promises You are greater than he is, and that You are greater within me than he is. You promised to deliver, defend, and protect me from my enemy. Your Word says You have given me power over all the power of my enemy, and nothing in any way harms me, in Jesus' name. Amen!

Scriptures for Meditation: Exodus 33:14; Psalm 71:21; Job 33:12; Psalm 59:1, AMP; Luke 10:19; 1 John 4:4

Chapter 13

❧

Casting ALL Our Cares!

*B*y the end of the year, the Lord had directed me to move. Four months later, Jason, Joel, and I, along with my parents, moved to another state and I was working for a local Christian ministry. While the custody battle was far from over, I had a newfound peace in just knowing that Greg was out of our lives—at least for the moment.

Three years after our last move it started again.

Following the gun incident, the boys and I had little to no contact with Greg for a while.

Relaxed and at peace, I had stopped praying about receiving full custody. Another way of putting it is that I let my spiritual guard down.

One day, a woman stood at the front door of our home holding some papers.

"Are you Linda Johnson?" she asked.

"Yes."

She then handed me the papers.

Greg had filed for custody of our children.

The Bible says in 1 Peter 5:6-7, "Humble yourselves therefore under the mighty hand of God, that he may exalt you in due time: casting all your care upon him; for he careth for you."

I had been praying and trusting the Lord through this entire situation. Now that it seemed like the walls were caving in on me from all sides, I had to hold on to God even closer and believe for and rely upon His protection. If I didn't truly put my trust in the Lord now, and keep it there, I knew there was no chance Jason,

Joel, and I could ever walk out of this horrible situation together victoriously. There was absolutely no way I would ever be able to survive this onslaught in my own strength.

I had to get another attorney, this time in my new state.

I remembered the story of the Israelites and how God delivered them from the tyranny of King Pharaoh, who had kept them bound for so many years. I thought about how, after being in slavery for so long, and with no hope in sight, the children of Israel suddenly found themselves walking out of bondage and into a new life of freedom by the demonstration of God's power. I'm sure many reading this book have heard the story and are very familiar with the miraculous way in which God stepped in and saved His people—how He heard the cries of His people and answered them by sending Moses to Pharaoh with the staunch directive to "Let My people go!"

After refusing a number of times to obey God, and watching his own people suffer as God put a series of plagues on Egypt, Pharaoh was finally convinced that God was serious and decided to do as God had commanded by releasing the Israelites. When Pharaoh changed his mind and decided to send his troops to retrieve the captives and bring them back to Egypt, God was right there to protect them and destroy the Egyptian army.

The entire story is one of inspiration and encouragement for anyone who finds themselves in a desperate situation. I'm encouraged every time I read the account of how God not only delivered His people from bondage, but how He made sure that their oppressors never bothered them again. The story is rather lengthy, but well worth reading. Here's a portion of it from Exodus 14:5-31 (NKJV):

> Now it was told the king of Egypt that the people had fled, and the heart of Pharaoh and his servants was turned against the people; and they said, "Why have we done this, that we have let Israel go from serving us?" So he made ready his chariot and took his people with him. Also, he took six hundred choice chariots, and all the chariots of Egypt with captains over every one of them. And the LORD

hardened the heart of Pharaoh king of Egypt, and he pursued the children of Israel; and the children of Israel went out with boldness. So the Egyptians pursued them, all the horses and chariots of Pharaoh, his horsemen and his army, and overtook them camping by the sea beside Pi Hahiroth, before Baal Zephon.

And when Pharaoh drew near, the children of Israel lifted their eyes, and behold, the Egyptians marched after them. So they were very afraid, and the children of Israel cried out to the LORD. Then they said to Moses, "Because *there were* no graves in Egypt, have you taken us away to die in the wilderness? Why have you so dealt with us, to bring us up out of Egypt? *Is* this not the word that we told you in Egypt, saying, 'Let us alone that we may serve the Egyptians?' For *it would have been* better for us to serve the Egyptians than that we should die in the wilderness."

And Moses said to the people, "Do not be afraid. Stand still, and see the salvation of the LORD, which He will accomplish for you today. For the Egyptians whom you see today, you shall see again no more forever. The LORD will fight for you, and you shall hold your peace."

And the LORD said to Moses, "Why do you cry to Me? Tell the children of Israel to go forward. But lift up your rod, and stretch out your hand over the sea and divide it. And the children of Israel shall go on *dry* ground through the midst of the sea. And I indeed will harden the hearts of the Egyptians, and they shall follow them. So I will gain honor over Pharaoh and over all his army, his chariots, and his horsemen. Then the Egyptians shall know that I *am* the LORD, when I have gained honor for Myself over Pharaoh, his chariots, and his horsemen."

And the Angel of God, who went before the camp of Israel, moved and went behind them; and the pillar of cloud went from before them and stood behind them. So it came between the camp of the Egyptians and the camp of Israel. Thus it was a cloud and darkness *to the one*, and it gave light by night *to the other,* so that the one did not come near the other all that night. Then Moses stretched out his hand over the sea; and the LORD caused the sea to go back by a strong east wind all that night, and made the sea into dry *land*, and the waters were divided. So the children of Israel went into the midst of the sea on the dry *ground*, and the waters *were* a wall to them on their right hand and on their left. And the Egyptians pursued and went after them into the midst of the sea, all Pharaoh's horses, his chariots, and his horsemen.

Now it came to pass, in the morning watch, that the LORD looked down upon the army of the Egyptians through the pillar of fire and cloud, and He troubled the army of the Egyptians. And He took off their chariot wheels, so that they drove them with difficulty; and the Egyptians said, "Let us flee from the face of Israel, for the LORD fights for them against the Egyptians."

Then the LORD said to Moses, "Stretch out your hand over the sea, that the waters may come back upon the Egyptians, on their chariots, and on their horsemen." And Moses stretched out his hand over the sea; and when the morning appeared, the sea returned to its full depth, while the Egyptians were fleeing into it. So the LORD overthrew the Egyptians in the midst of the sea. Then the waters returned and covered the chariots, the horsemen, *and* all the army of Pharaoh that came into the sea after them. Not so much as one of them remained. But the children of Israel had walked on dry *land* in the midst of the sea, and the waters were a wall to them on their right hand and on their left.

So the LORD saved Israel that day out of the hand of the Egyptians, and Israel saw the Egyptians dead on the seashore. Thus Israel saw the great work which the LORD had done in Egypt; so the people feared the LORD, and believed the LORD and His servant Moses.

"So the Lord saved Linda and her sons that day out of the hands of an abusive situation."

Personally, I believed that's what the Lord was speaking to

me through that passage of scripture. That passage of scripture is a powerfully revealing testimony of God's compassionate desire and willingness not only to deliver us when we are in trouble, but of His ability to protect us along the way. Remembering God's faithfulness to deliver His people from what appeared to be an impossible situation, gave me the faith I needed to continue to pursue my cause. It gave me the strength to fight for my children and their safety.

At that point, I became even more determined than ever that I was going to win the battle—that I would have full and complete custody of Jason and Joel. Once and for all, we would be delivered from Greg's tyranny that had haunted us for years.

Another Round with the Courts

Greg decided to move to our area. With him living nearby, it created different challenges than we ever had before.

Both Greg and I were ordered by the court to submit to psychological testing, part of which was to determine our mental stability and whether we were fit to raise Jason and Joel. Meanwhile, there was another caveat. Fearing their son could possibly lose all rights to his children, Greg's parents sued for custody of Jason and Joel. If fighting one custody battle wasn't enough, now I was facing two!

This new threat introduced more problems, including the harassment of a private investigator who literally stalked me. I would see a black pickup truck parked outside my house at all hours of the day or night. I never learned who was inside the truck, but the person followed me to and from work every day for several weeks.

Of course, the addition of a second custody suit meant more time in court, which meant more money for attorney fees, which I didn't have. But I refused to fear. I kept my faith strong in the Lord. God had remained faithful to me, and He would continue to do so. Now was not the time to doubt, to look at circumstances and question God's ability to help and deliver me. He did it for the Israelites, He would do it for me and my children.

It seemed like there was money going out in every direction. We had to pay for a social study; our sons were ordered to have a guardian ad litem (which is a fancy name for their own attorney), and I had to pay half of that expense; and a deposition was required, which meant even more money. I still had to keep current on my attorney fees, and my ex-husband was not paying child support.

God's Word had to be my final authority.

I believed I would receive full custody of Jason and Joel.

I continued to receive encouragement from people around me, and even through various ministers and friends.

The Bible says in Proverbs 27:17, "Iron sharpeneth iron; so a man sharpeneth the countenance of his friend." And in Psalm 119:105, David described God's Word as a "lamp unto my feet, and a light unto my path."

When you're in trouble and don't know what to do or which way to turn, the Word of God and His Holy Spirit will direct you. They will shine light on the entire situation and show you, step by step, what to do, where to go, and how to get there. Some situations are easier than others, and some don't take a long time to maneuver through. The key is trusting God, believing His Word, and exercising patience.

I know what hearing God's words of encouragement from others did, and continues to do for me, and I want to do everything I possibly can to help and encourage others who are where I was. Here are just a few of the things I heard:

"Keep a right mental attitude!"
"When you plan to stand forever, your victory will come."
"Only say the Word!"
"Choose life so you and your seed shall live (Deuteronomy 30:19)."
"Continue to praise the Lord. Praise silences the avenger and the enemy."
"You are released from this matter."
"Walk by faith, not by sight."
"No Word, no faith."

After hearing such encouraging words, my faith suddenly became supercharged. My strength was renewed like that of an eagle. I found myself ready to go—to press on and see how God was going to work this out. Actually, I pretty much already knew the answer to that. I knew from the very beginning that I would end up with my sons—getting full custody. I just didn't know when or how I would get there.

During one court session, the judge ordered that Jason and Joel were to spend the day with their dad. It was the first time they had seen Greg since the gun incident, and Jason told me later that he was really scared to be with his dad.

"I called on the Lord and I saw our angels there to protect us," Jason told me.

From that point on, I reminded myself daily of those things I had heard. I saw Jason, Joel, myself, and our situation in a totally different and more encouraging light. Giving up and quitting was not an option for me. I had come too far and fought much too long and hard to see everything taken away. My children were a big part of my life. I was not about to fail them or lose them. Each day, I confessed these words: "I am what the Word says I am. I can do what the Word says I can do. I can have what the Word says I can have. I am not moved by what I see. I am not moved by what I feel. I expect a miracle today."

They weren't just words coming out of my mouth. They were what I felt, what I knew in my heart to be the truth. And I was not about to back down from them.

Brother Roberts would have been pleased to know that, years after hearing him say it, I was still believing and speaking those words that had become such a powerful part of my life, and I'm sure the lives of thousands of others: "Something good is going to happen to you."

———— ⌘ ————

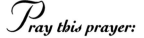*ray this prayer:*

Dear Father, my enemy has incited others against me. They all are lying and trying to discredit me. They are threatening to

take me to court, to make me appear incompetent and guilty, but I am not afraid or terrified because You are with me. You promise to go with me, to fight for me against all my enemies, and to save me. Thank You for knowing my heart and my innocence. I am in peace and my conscience is clear, and although I am stirred up against their accusations, charges, and lies against me, I choose not to fret because of them. I choose to rest in You because You are mighty in battle, and this battle is Yours. Thank You for proving my innocence and my enemies' guilt. I cast the care of this court battle into Your mighty and capable hands, in Jesus' name. Amen!

Scriptures for Meditation: Deuteronomy 20:1-4; Acts 24:16; Proverbs 24:19; Psalm 24:8; 1 Samuel 17:47; Psalm 37:1-40; Isaiah 55:11; Psalm 91:8; Psalm 23:1-6

Chapter 14

❧

The Pendulum Slows to a HALT!

I once read an account of a college student who had been given a class assignment to prepare a lesson for his speech class. During his presentation, which he titled "The Law of the Pendulum," the student carefully outlined the physical principle that governed the swinging pendulum.

The law of the pendulum, he explained, is that a pendulum can never return to a point higher than the point from which it was released. Because of friction and gravity, when the pendulum returns, it will fall short of its original release point. Each time it swings, the pendulum makes less and less of an arc, until finally it is at rest—a point which is known as the state of equilibrium, where all forces acting on the pendulum are equal.

If you can envision the pendulum on a grandfather clock, careful to notice its gradual decline in speed as it swings back and forth, then you can very quickly get an idea of what this student was describing in his research. The idea is that at whatever point the pendulum began, it will never return there again. As long as someone continues to wind up the clock, the pendulum will continue to sway back and forth. But unless someone steps in to manually pull it back to its original starting point, it will not swing that high again. And if no one winds up the clock, eventually the pendulum will come to a halt. It will stop completely!

A swinging pendulum!

For nearly fourteen years, that's what my life had been like.

Only, there was one difference.

More times than not, it seemed that the problems I faced were

ALWAYS at an all-time high. They never seemed to slow down. Every episode was like an escalation of the one before, with no end in sight.

The threats from Greg just wouldn't go away.

And the courtroom battles went from bad to worse.

Even the judge handling our case didn't seem to want to play fair. At one point when I was sitting on the witness stand, for instance, he turned, pointed his finger at me and said very angrily: "You will lose your children!" I tried not to let his words bother me, but how could I not? After all, he was the judge who would eventually decide the fate of my children.

This was the lowest point in my life. I immediately started meditating on the Word of God that I had already put into my heart. Yes, it didn't look like it was possible, at that point, for me to obtain full custody of my children. But I didn't go by what the judge said. I stood on the Word that God was telling me. I was convinced, and said: "That is subject to change!"

Greg and his attorneys accused me of "Parental Alienation Syndrome," saying I was deliberately trying to alienate the boys from their father.

When Greg's attorneys tried to prevent Jason from telling in court how his dad had put a gun to his neck, the judge ruled that, at age fifteen, Jason was grown up and mature enough to speak for himself. But when Jason's story sounded much like what I had testified earlier about Greg holding me at gunpoint, Greg's attorneys objected. They suggested that I had rehearsed with Jason what he should say on the witness stand. The judge seemed to agree. Of course, it wasn't true. Jason and I knew what had happened. He didn't need any coaxing.

Greg made every attempt to try and reconnect with the boys. I suppose he thought his being nice could turn things in his favor regarding custody. But that battle had long been lost. Although they were still very young, Jason and Joel had very strong recall regarding the abuse and bad treatment they had suffered at the hands of their dad. They didn't want to even talk with him, let alone be near him, and they made that point clear to me.

When the boys would tell me they didn't want to talk with

their father, Greg accused me of turning them against him. Joel said to me, "When I talk to my dad, it makes me feel dirty. Please don't make me talk to him."

Once during a conversation I had with Jason about how abusive Greg was when we talked over the phone, Jason told me, "Mom, you need to record these phone calls. You need to hear how bad it really is and what we have to put up with." Taking his advice, I later recorded several of my conversations with Greg. I also recorded conversations Greg had with Jason, which turned out be very revealing. Here's a portion of what Greg said to Jason during a particular conversation:

> "If you refuse to be with me, I will file contempt papers with the court. I guarantee you it's going to happen. It's not me that's going to put your mom in jail—it's you, Jason. If she don't obey the court order, then you've made the decision not to come with me, and that puts her in jail. You're the one that's going to put her in jail. I'm going to file the court papers. And that's it…I'll be there Saturday to pick you up at eight o'clock. And if you don't get in the car with me, I guarantee you I'm going to go home and I'm going to call my attorneys and I'm going to file papers with the court. That's just going to happen."

In case you're wondering why I didn't include Jason's response to what Greg was saying, it's because there was no response. With the exception of telling his dad not to call him any more and, at one point, telling Greg he was "pushing us farther and farther away from you," Jason remained silent during the conversation. Finally, Jason just hung up on his dad.

Greg's attorneys were pushing for a jury trial in hopes that they could get a jury to side with him, but my attorney suggested we try mediation. I had spoken with a number of mothers across the country down through the years regarding custody battles, and they all pretty much had the same grim report—they each had lost their child or children to their former husbands.

Up to this point, there wasn't *one* mother who had obtained full custody of her child or children. To my delight, as if I really had anything to be happy about at this point, Greg and his attorney agreed to try mediation. This meant that mediation would take the place of court, which meant there would be no courtroom involvement.

As part of the mediation, my attorney presented the transcribed documents of Greg's phone conversations with the boys. It was discovered and reported that Greg was trying to blame all of his conduct on me, the mother of his children. He was claiming that I intentionally alienated the children or asserted undue influence over them. But after reviewing the transcript of conversations the boys had with their father, it was revealed to the mediator that it was actually the other way around—that Greg had been alienating his own children.

The mediator wasn't pleased to hear this report. He then ordered counseling for the four of us. Sometimes it was me and the boys or Greg and the boys. I'm not sure why, but Greg and I never were asked to attend a session in which it was just the counselor, he, and me. Our family counselor advised that Joel should not be alone with Greg during any visitations.

The weekly mediation sessions meant more money out of my pocket. But that was okay. I knew that, somehow, God would provide. The important thing was that I STILL had my children.

———— ∞∞∞ ————

*P*ray this prayer:

Dear Father, lies and more lies have been spoken against me. I feel sad and disheartened. My enemies have twisted and shaded the truth so much to convince others that I am a hypocrite and a liar. How unfortunate that a person's innocence or guilt rests in the conclusions and judgments of others. Thank You for being my defense and my judge. I trust You to save me, in Jesus' name. Amen!

Scriptures for Meditation: Ezekiel 13:22; 1 Timothy 4:1-2; Psalm 94:22; Isaiah 33:22; Isaiah 54:17; Galatians 6:9; Isaiah 41:10-13

Chapter 15

❧

Justice Means 'Just Us'

Never pay back evil with more evil. Do things in such a way that everyone can see you are honorable. Do all that you can to live in peace with everyone. Dear friends, never take revenge. Leave that to the righteous anger of God. For the Scriptures say, "I will take revenge; I will pay them back," says the LORD.

— Romans 12:17-19, New Living Translation

I can remember it as though it happened yesterday.

It was on a Friday. The sun shone brightly, and the temperatures hovered around the mid to upper 70s. It was one of those days that I would have loved to just forget about housework, curl up in front of the TV with my sons and watch a movie, or go on a family bike ride.

Only it wasn't my weekend to have them.

Greg had arrived and was anxious for the boys to load their stuff into the truck so he could leave to begin their weekend visitation. As usual, Jason and Joel were less than thrilled at having to be with him.

Greg's short visit with me was cordial.

Jason was to perform in a concert on Saturday night. Greg and I agreed to meet before the concert and that I would bring Jason's instrument and a change of clothes. When Joel announced that he wanted to attend the birthday party of a friend, Greg became angry. He shouted "No!" to Joel, and then told the boys to get in the truck so they could leave.

I quickly went into the house.

They sat on our lawn for hours that night, refusing to go with their dad for the weekend. After much persuasion by Greg, the boys finally went with him. I didn't understand then, but after hearing later the recorded phone conversations Greg had with the boys, I understood why they got into his vehicle that day. Greg had told them if they refused to go with him, then he would call his attorney and have contempt papers filed against me with the court. As Greg reinforced it to Jason, it would have been Jason who would have put me, his mom, in jail because he didn't get into his truck. That was a lot of pressure to put on Jason or anyone! Jason didn't know if what Greg was saying was true or not. Because of his love and concern for me, he chose to go with his dad.

For reasons I'm still not clear about to this day, Jason never made it to his concert.

A Sudden Change of Heart

The following Sunday evening, I was sitting by the window waiting for Jason and Joel to return when Greg's pickup truck pulled up and stopped on the street in front of the house. Jason and Joel stepped out on the passenger side, and then I noticed something rolling out of the truck. Greg literally tossed the boys' belongings out of the truck and drove off.

A few days later, I received a phone call from Greg while at work telling me he didn't want to continue to force the boys to spend time with him for visitations. He then asked me to have my attorney draw up legal papers that would stop his child support payments and visitation rights, and that he would agree to my having full custody of Jason and Joel.

FULL CUSTODY!

Did I hear that right?

Lord, what is going on? Can this be true? Am I hearing what I think I'm hearing?

A thousand questions were racing through my mind as I tried to remain calm, and answer Greg in the most civil, professional way possible. Inside, my heart was pounding out the beats of a thousand drums.

Finally, it was happening!

The pendulum that had swung so high, for so long, was about to slow its swing. The roller-coaster ride was coming to an end. Finally, I was about to see the salvation of the Lord in our lives like I had never seen it before!

Just as he had done for the children of Israel, God was about to do it for me and my children! Or was this another one of Greg's tricks? He had done so many ruthless and manipulative things to me over the past fourteen years that I just couldn't be sure. I didn't want to take a chance and find myself back in court with no real defense.

A week later, Greg called again, this time asking if I had consulted my attorney about how much it would cost to have the papers drawn up.

"If you're serious about this, then send your request to me in writing."

He did.

The following week, Greg called again wanting to know what it would cost to finalize the papers and grant me full custody of Jason and Joel. He was trying to decide whether to remain where he was or move back home, he said, and wanted the matter resolved. It was estimated that he was over $30,000 behind in support payments, so I suggested he pay all the court costs.

The final week of October, Greg, my attorney, and I stood outside the courtroom waiting for our case to be called. The judge presiding over the court was the same judge who, just a year earlier, had pointed his finger at me in trepidation and declared that I would lose my two sons.

As we waited our turn, the compassion and love of Jesus rose up in me toward Greg. I didn't hate this man. This was not the same man I married eighteen years ago. I reinforced to him the truth that, no matter what, God still loved him.

Moments later, Greg and I had signed the papers. The court had made its final declaration, and suddenly it was over.

Jason and Joel were in school. But soon, they would know. Soon, everyone would know. Finally, it was over!

The pendulum that had swung for so long was swinging no more.

That night, my mind raced back over the last fourteen years, and particularly the last ten years. Tears began to fill my eyes. I was so thankful how the Lord had delivered us. All the praise and glory goes to Him. I could not have done it without Him. From all the mothers I had spoken with, I was the first mother who obtained full custody of her children. That was the favor of God!

In that still, quiet moment, those words came back to me: "Yes, my daughter, have not I seen you? Do I not know your down sitting and your uprising?" saith the Lord. "You are a mighty woman of valor, because you'll not give up."

"Because you'll not give up."

No, I had not given up. I had never quit. And because I didn't quit, because I put my trust in a God who always keeps His Word, and I kept it there, He never quit on me. God was faithful to do exactly what He promised me in His Word. He kept us safe, and He delivered us from the enemy.

He had won the battle for me and my sons, and had given us the victory! I was reminded of this verse: "Now thanks *be* unto God, who ALWAYS causeth us to triumph in Christ" (2 Corinthians 2:14, emphasis added).

---

*P*ray this prayer:

Dear Father, throughout this long ordeal, fear, discouragement, hopelessness, and darkness have tried to oppress me. They have pressed in heavily against me. But, thanks be to You because by Your grace through faith, I have trusted You, and I have believed Your Word. And, just as You have promised, You have not disappointed my hope and faith in You, nor have You allowed my enemies to triumph over me! In fact, You have made my enemies to be at peace with me because You have approved of my life. The light of Your presence has arisen upon me, and the light of Your Word has shown me the right pathway. You have renewed my strength and You have caused me to triumph in Christ Jesus! You have won a great victory for us, in Jesus' name! Amen!

Scriptures for Meditation: Psalm 25:2; Proverbs 16:7 MSG. Isaiah 60:2; Psalm 119:105; Isaiah 40:31; 2 Corinthians 2:14; 2 Samuel 23:10

Epilogue

*On the morning of November 2, 1987, New York City police
responded to a 9-1-1 call from Hedda (Nussbaum). Entering the
Greenwich Village apartment that Hedda shared with her common-law husband, wealthy attorney Joel Steinberg, police found
the couple's illegally adopted daughter, Lisa, beaten and unconscious. Hedda and Joel were arrested. Six-year-old Lisa died on
November 5. Prosecutors eventually dropped the charges against
Hedda. Joel was charged with second-degree murder and first-
degree manslaughter, convicted of manslaughter in 1988 after a
televised trial that included seven days of chilling testimony from
Hedda. Joel was given a sentence of eight-and-a-third to twenty-
five years, and is due to be released from prison in June of next
year.*

Those were the words of then TV talk show host Larry King
as he introduced a segment of his *Larry King Live* TV show
in June 2003. The segment featured an interview with Hedda
Nussbaum, and focused on the famed court trial of 1989 in which
her common-law husband had been convicted of beating their
six-year-old *illegally* adopted daughter, Lisa Steinberg, to death.
In a widely-publicized trial that received national attention in
1989, including being featured on the cover of *People* magazine,
testimony revealed that Hedda, a once successful children's book
editor, had for years been repeatedly and brutally battered and
beaten by Steinberg, who forced her into a life of drugs.

During her testimony, Nussbaum told of being systematically
brainwashed and humiliated by Steinberg over a dozen years,
beaten so many times that she required at least three plastic sur-
geries to reconstruct her face. Nussbaum testified that while her
child lay unconscious for twelve hours, Steinberg refused to let
her summon help and ordered her to freebase cocaine with him.

Not once did Hedda ever report the abuse to authorities.

And not once did she reach out for help. When asked during the interview if there were any part of her that said, "I could have prevented Lisa's death," Nussbaum told King:

"...There are times when, I think, I wish I had done such and such. But I understand now very clearly why I didn't, and I do give the blame to Joel Steinberg. I mean, of course, I wish, you know, I had, you know, had run away with her, that I had stabbed him with a knife, done anything."

In the years following Lisa's death, Nussbaum co-facilitated a group for battered women and later worked as a paralegal for a group that assists battered women. In 1995, she began giving lectures about abuse. When Steinberg was released from prison in 2004, Nussbaum dropped out of the public's eye until after the release of a book she had written about the abuse. Nussbaum also changed her name.

'If Only I Had Said Something!'

The old saying that "hindsight is 20/20" is true. But in truth, no one should ever have to look back on a situation that involves abuse, whether to a child or an adult, and have to utter those regretful words. Reaching out is THE most important thing anyone can do to stop the abuse.

Though I knew that, I didn't act on it at first.

Today, I wish that I had.

But more importantly, I'm thankful that I finally did something.

As parents, we have been given the great responsibility to nurture, provide for, and protect our children. I didn't start out on this journey expecting to face emotional, verbal, and physical terror that nearly destroyed the lives of my sons and myself. The truth is, no one does. But when those things do surface, it's important to know that God is your best friend. There's hope and comfort in knowing that no matter how bad it looks, or how difficult it seems to be, God ALWAYS makes a way of escape.

Some might say that my story is not much different from those of hundreds of thousands of others worldwide. And in a sense, they are correct. But the truth is, every person's story is different in its own right. And every story deserves to be told for the sake of helping the next victim. I suppose that's the reason I wanted to write this book.

I know the heartache, pain, and suffering my sons and I endured. Years have now passed and, thankfully, by God's love and grace, Jason, Joel, and I are in the process of healing and recovery. Yes, we have forgiven, but on the other hand, we have not forgotten. Life goes on and so do we—step by step, and day by day.

Abuse is a terrible thing. It is a deadly thing. It's something no person, female or male, adult or child, young or old, should ever have to suffer.

It is my prayer that, after reading this book, you will agree. And if you are a victim, you will take steps to get help—TODAY!

Final Thoughts

Standing on the Promises of God's Word

Throughout my ordeal, I stood firm on a number of scriptures from God's Word, including this one from the Romans 4:17-21, which declares the faith of Abraham:

"(As it is written, I have made thee a father of many nations,) before him whom he believed, *even* God, who quickeneth the dead, and calleth those things which be not as though they were. Who against hope believed in hope, that he might become the father of many nations, according to that which was spoken, So shall thy seed be. And being not weak in faith, he considered not his own body now dead, when he was about an hundred years old, neither yet the deadness of Sarah's womb: He staggered not at the promise of God through unbelief; but was strong in faith, giving glory to God; and being fully persuaded that, what he had promised, he was able also to perform."

John 20:24-29 reads:

"But Thomas, one of the twelve, called Didymus, was not with them when Jesus came. The other disciples therefore said unto him, We have seen the Lord. But he said unto them, Except I shall see in his hands the print of the nails, and put my finger into the print of the nails, and thrust my hand into his side, I will not believe. And after eight days again his disciples were within, and Thomas with them: then came Jesus, the doors being shut, and stood in the midst, and said, Peace be unto you. Then saith he to Thomas, Reach hither thy finger, and behold my hands; and reach hither thy hand, and thrust it into my side: and

be not faithless, but believing. And Thomas answered
and said unto him, My Lord and my God. Jesus saith
unto him, Thomas, because thou hast seen me, thou hast
believed: blessed are they that have not seen, and yet
have believed."

Thomas' faith was based on physical evidence. He had to see
the holes in Jesus' hands before he would believe it was Him. He
wanted to only believe what he could see. Jesus instructed him,
"Blessed are those who have not seen and yet have believed."

Had Abraham gone by what he could see and what his
physical senses told him, he would have never received God's
promise. Common sense tells us that a man and a woman in
their nineties are not likely to have children. Yet, Abraham had
God's promise that he was to be the "father of many nations."
Abraham's faith was based on that promise. He didn't believe his
feelings; he didn't believe according to what he saw; he didn't
believe his physical senses. He believed God's promise.

As followers of Jesus Christ, the blessing of Abraham also
belongs to us: "That the blessing of Abraham might come on the
Gentiles through Jesus Christ; that we might receive the promise of
the Spirit through faith" (Galatians 3:14). Galatians 3:29 says, "And
if ye be Christ's, then are ye Abraham's seed, and heirs according
to the promise." Since we are Abraham's seed, his blessings ought
to be ours, because we belong to Christ. We receive the blessing the
same way Abraham received it: through faith.

I could not stagger in my faith. I could not afford to be like
Thomas, who was filled with doubt and unbelief. I had to be *fully
persuaded* that what God promised in His Word, He was more
than able to perform—that He would give us the victory and I
would receive full custody! With renewed faith and hope, I had
to continue to stand for the promise, just as Abraham did. I had
to keep speaking the Word of God to our situation, believing that
I had full custody of my sons, in Jesus' name! I could not go by
how things looked. I had to be patient and keep believing that
God's Word would change our circumstances, even while the
battle was still raging around us.

I learned the importance of living by faith, and was told the four key elements necessary to live by faith: First, you have to study and meditate God's Word; second, you must believe God's Word; third, you must not consider the contradictory circumstances; and fourth, you must always give God praise.

When you apply these four elements, then you are certain to receive whatever you ask from God as long as it agrees with His Word.

That's just part of the lesson to be learned. Never talk the problem—only the answer or solution from God's Word. Find scriptures that cover your circumstances and you have a solid foundation for faith. Say only what you want to come to pass, according to God's promise, and don't worry! Worry doesn't change anything. It doesn't change your circumstances; it only makes the situation worse. Declare from the beginning what your end result will be. Declare your victory!

Romans 10:8-9 says: "But what saith it? The word is nigh thee, *even* in thy mouth, and in thy heart: that is, the word of faith, which we preach; that if thou shalt confess with thy mouth the Lord Jesus, and shalt believe in thine heart that God hath raised him from the dead, thou shalt be saved." Based on these verses, you should confess with your mouth and believe in your heart that Jesus was raised from the dead and then you will be saved. Faith has to be in two places: in your mouth and in your heart.

Then, in verse 10 we read, "For with the heart man believeth unto righteousness; and with the mouth confession is made unto salvation."

Through these verses we can see the importance of speaking what you want to come to pass.

The Bible goes on to say in Ephesians 2:8, "For by grace are ye saved through faith, and that not of yourselves; it is the gift of God." It is *by grace* and *through faith* that you receive the victory. You can't have one without the other. *Grace* and *faith* work together.

What is grace? It is a gift from God. It is something we don't earn. We receive it by faith. You depend on God for His strength, wisdom, deliverance, peace, mercy, or whatever the Bible promises you. Hebrews 4:16 says, "Let us therefore come boldly unto the throne of grace, that we may obtain mercy, and find grace to help in time of need."

In my situation, I found *grace to escape.*

What is faith? Hebrews 11:1 says, "Now faith is the substance of things hoped for, the evidence of things not seen." Verse 6 continues, "But without faith it is impossible to please him, for he who comes to God must believe that he is, and that he is a rewarder of those that diligently seek him."

We have to have faith to please God.

How do we get faith? "So then faith cometh by hearing, and hearing by the word of God" (Romans 10:17). Faith doesn't come by someone praying for you. Faith comes by you hearing the Word of God.

How do we use or release our faith? The following verses from Mark, chapter 11, tell us:

"Have faith in God" (v. 22). The Bible says the just shall live by faith.

"For verily I *say* unto you, That whosoever shall *say* unto this mountain, Be thou removed and be thou cast into the sea; and shall not doubt in his heart, but shall believe that those things which he *saith* shall come to pass, he shall have whatsoever he *saith*" (v. 23). Faith has to continue to speak to the mountain. It is saying words that you believe in your heart.

"What things soever ye desire when you pray, believe that ye receive them, and ye shall have them" (v. 24). Jesus said to believe that you receive the things you desire when you pray. Faith is believing what the Word of God says about your situation—it is saying words that you believe in your heart.

Faith speaks (Romans 10:6). You just can't think it and have it come to pass. You must say it consistently. Someone reading this right now may be thinking in their heart, *I'll never win my battle. I might as well just give up!*

Don't give up! (Galatians 6:9, paraphrased). That's what the enemy wants you to do. He wants you to turn your eyes away from God, away from His Word, and look at the circumstances.

He wants you to crumble in fear and unbelief. Don't talk defeat. That's not what God wants, and it's not what His Word says.

Today could be the day of your breakthrough.

"Let us not be weary in well doing, for in due season we shall reap, if we *don't give up*" (Galatians 6:9, paraphrased).

Stand on God's Word. Believe what His Word says and speak it out of your mouth. When you speak the Word of God, it will cut off the head of your circumstance or situation. His Word will *not* return void, but will always accomplish what it was sent out to do (Isaiah 55:11). You can go into the enemy's camp and rescue your children from his hands and never leave your house. How do you do that? By speaking the Word of God over your situation. Keep the Word of God in abundance when the storm is raging and when you are tempted to throw in the towel and quit. The Word of God is ALWAYS your answer.

First John 5:4 says, "...this is the victory that overcometh the world, *even* our faith."

"For we walk by faith, not by sight" (2 Corinthians 5:7).

During our marriage and divorce, my husband threatened me several times by saying, "I am going to take the children and you will never see them again." The devil made sure those words, above all others, echoed in my mind. When I experienced any form of fear, the two scriptures I was encouraged to read and meditate on *several* times a day were 2 Corinthians 10:5, "Casting down imaginations, and every high thing that exalteth itself against the knowledge of God, and bringing into captivity every thought to the obedience of Christ," and Philippians 4:8: "Think on things that are true, honest, just, pure, lovely, of a good report, if there be any virtue or praise, think only on these things" (paraphrased). When I would say this verse, I added the word "only": "I ONLY think on these things."

Keep feeding your faith by reading the Word of God. God will make a way of escape for you. Fight the good fight of faith (1 Timothy 6:12). This fight is a good fight. You have to be 100 percent committed to stand by faith. You cannot have faith and fear at the same time. You will either have one or the other. Your faith has to be in the Lord Jesus Christ. You must have faith in God's Word. You can't put your trust in others—not even yourself. You must trust God.

The key is to keep the Word of God before your eyes and in your ears. Sometimes, you will have to turn off the television, or turn away from other distractions so you can stay focused on the Word and meditate God's answers. According to Joshua 1:8, meditating on God's Word is what leads you to success and prosperity. Verse 9 says, "Be strong and of good courage; do not be afraid, nor be dismayed, for the Lord your God is with you wherever you go" (paraphrased).

Going to church on Sunday will not win your battle. You need to read the Word of God concerning your situation every day. Encourage yourself in the Lord. Thank Him for your victory in advance.

Nearly everywhere I turn, I hear the cries of hurting parents and children facing situations similar to ours and they don't know what to do. They seem to have lost their hope. They need to realize that it is *never* too late to believe for a favorable outcome. The devil doesn't have any new plots or ideas. His mission is to kill, steal, and destroy the lives of you and your children, and that's what he intends to do (John 10:10). He wants parents to give up and believe his lies. He uses fear as a weapon. Put the devil on the run with the Word of God.

Satan uses persecution to stop you from believing you receive your victory. Why does persecution come? To steal the Word of God, get you off the Word and away from your promise. (Read Mark 4 about the parable of the sower.) You must sow the Word. Farmers sow seeds. Believers sow the Word of God.

In 2 Corinthians 12:9, the Word sums up all that God has for you, and everything He is willing to do for you. God promised Apostle Paul: "My grace is sufficient for thee: for my strength is made perfect in weakness." And Paul responded: "Most gladly therefore will I rather glory in my infirmities, that the power of Christ may rest upon me."

God's grace is sufficient to bring you through anything. *His grace is amazing!*

When Jason and Joel turned eighteen, they each legally had

their last name changed. They refused to be called by the same last name as their dad. Jason had to stand before the same judge who had told me that I would lose my children. It was the same judge who granted me full custody of my two sons. And now, this same judge was approving Jason's name change.

God is faithful, and He *will always* work on your behalf. Let Him work for you as He worked for Abraham, for others in the Bible, and as He did for us. He has given you great and precious promises, and He always keeps His Word. Trust Him to help you, and never give up!

CPSIA information can be obtained at www.ICGtesting.com
Printed in the USA
LVOW102136290413

331452LV00003B/11/P